GENERAL ROBERT E.

MW01293192

Judith McGuire

GENERAL ROBERT E. LEE, THE CHRISTIAN SOLDIER

Published by Firework Press

New York City, NY

First published 1873

Copyright © Firework Press, 2015

All rights reserved

ABOUT FIREWORK PRESS

Firework Press prints and publishes the greatest books about American history ever written, including seminal works written by our nation's most influential figures.

THIS little volume has been prepared by a lady of Virginia, at the request of a few Christian men who have deeply revered and heartily loved the character of General Robert E. Lee.

Looking upon him as a very high type of manhood, they have desired that his testimony to the truth of Christianity, and the example and teaching of his life, so, single-hearted, so clear, so eloquent in behalf of duty, of virtue, and of religion, should be as widely influential and as effective as possible.

Until, in the course of Providence, sectional animosity in this country culminated in fury, and great questions of state were referred to the arbitrament of the sword, there was no man who stood so fairly in the eyes of the whole American people, or who had so sure and unquestioned a title to their esteem and affection, as General Lee. That he deplored the separation he could not prevent, is clear enough. That his own determination and course were based upon a high sense of duty, none can doubt. In the great crisis that was upon us, wealth, honor, life to him were as nothing. The question of duty was all in all. Deciding that in favor of his native State, he abandoned everything, forsook the strong, and gave himself heart and soul to what, none better than he knew, was the weaker side. Whether he was right or wrong, God knows. The honesty of his purpose and his magnanimity the whole world has approved

The principles of his character, the motives of his actions, and his fidelity to Christian responsibilities, may be admired, regardless of politics and sectional differences. In these he glorified God; for these he will be admired and loved the world over; and for these he is commended to the young people of America.

CHAPTER I.BIRTH AND ANCESTRY.

ROBERT EDWARD LEE, our Christian soldier and brave leader to many victories, "was born at Stratford, in Westmoreland County, Virginia, on the 19th of January, 1807." This entry is found in the family Bible in his mother's handwriting. His family, of Norman descent, is traced by himself, in his sketch of his father's life, to Launcelot Lee of Loudon, in France, who accompanied William the Conqueror to England. After the battle of Hastings, he, with other followers, was rewarded by the Conqueror with lands wrested from the Saxons. All that we know is, that his estate was in Essex, England. From that time his name is found, ever and anon, in English annals, and always in honorable connection.

Thus, we next find Lionel Lee accompanying King Richard the Lion-hearted, in the year 1192, in his third Crusade to rescue the Holy Land from the followers of Mohammed. There, his career was marked by gallantry, and at the siege of Acre he received a solid proof of the approbation of his king. On his return to England, he was made first Earl of Litchfield, and was presented by the king with the estate of Ditchley—which name, centuries afterwards, his descendants gave to an estate in Northumberland County, Virginia.

In 1542, Richard Lee accompanied the Earl of Surry in his unfortunate expedition across the Scottish border. Two of the family are found about the same time to have so distinguished themselves as to have their banners suspended in St, George's Chapel, in Windsor Castle, with the Lee coat of arms about them. These incidents show that the blood of our hero was as valiant as it was virtuous, and the motto which accompanied the coat of arms of his ancestors, "Non incantus futuri," seems, says one of his biographers, to have been descriptive of one of the traits of their great descendant.

In the reign of Charles the First, we find the family of Lee in Shropshire, and of the cavalier stock. Then it was that Richard Lee, described as a gentleman of many accomplishments, determined to come to the New World, of which he had heard such marvellous accounts. Bishop Meade, in his book on the "Old Churches and Families of Virginia," says of him, "He was a man of good stature, comely visage, enterprising genius, a sound head, vigorous spirit, and generous nature. When he got to Virginia, which was at that time very little cultivated, he was so much pleased with the country that he made large settlements with the servants he brought over." He returned again and again to England, but finally settled between the Potomac and Rappahannock rivers, in the country known as the Northern Neck of Virginia. He was for a long time Secretary of the Commonwealth, under Sir William Berkeley, Governor, and is said to have exercised much influence upon the Colony in that great revolution which made Cromwell supreme in England. He died in Virginia, leaving one son, Richard, who remained in this country, and was distinguished as a man of much learning. Henry, the fifth son of this Richard Lee, was the ancestor of General R. E. Lee. He married a Miss Bland, and their third son, Henry, married a Miss Grymes, and became the father of General Henry Lee, of the old Revolution, known as "Light Horse Harry," because he so successfully led the cavalry against Tarleton and Cornwallis in the Southern campaign. He (Light Horse Harry) first married his cousin Matilda, a lady, it is said, of great beauty, whom her husband lovingly called the "divine Matilda." She was daughter of Philip Ludwell Lee, of Stratford, where, after the Revolution, he resided with his father-in-law; and by this marriage he became possessed of this family residence. His first wife having died, he married, on the

18th of June, 1793, Anne Hill Carter, a daughter of Charles Carter, Esq., of Shirley, on James River, a gentleman of wealth and high position, who was renowned for his benevolence; which trait seems to have been inherited by his grandson to a remarkable degree. Robert Edward Lee was the second son of this marriage.

The stately old mansion, Stratford, was originally built by the first Richard Lee who came to this country; it was afterwards destroyed by fire while the residence of his grandson Thomas, who was the fourth son of the learned Richard. He at once determined to rebuild it. He was a member of the King's Council, and so much was he esteemed both in the Colonies and in England, that the Government and merchants immediately contributed to defray the expense of reconstructing it; and it is said that Queen Caroline, the wife of George the Second, united largely in tile subscription from her private purse. The immense stricture soon arose, at a cost of about eighty thousand dollars. It still stands in Westmoreland County, on a picturesque bluff overlooking the Potomac, with its thick walls of English brick, its immense hall, its antique corridors, its wide saloon, its pavilions, balustrades, and clusters of chimneys, its extensive lawn, with ancient oaks, forest poplars, cedars, and maples, with the occasional Lombardy poplar, which has doubtless, with its towering and pointed top, attracted many a weary traveller to the refined hospitalities of Stratford; but alas! alas! it has long ago passed from the ownership of the Lees. The chamber in which Robert E. Lee was born was the same ill which his renowned relatives Richard Henry and Francis Lightfoot Lee first saw the light. Within five miles of Stratford stood "Pope's Creek," the birthplace of Washington.

CHAPTER II.REMOVAL OF HIS FAMILY TO ALEXANDRIA.

THE father of General Lee removed to Alexandria, for the purpose of educating his children, when Robert was but four years of age, but the peaceful, quiet, country scenes left a deep impression upon his childish imagination. He always loved the country, loved horses and country pursuits; the trees, streams and grass were dearer to him than all the elegancies and grandeur of the most refined city life. During the last year of his life, he said to a lady, "Nothing does me as much good as to visit my son at the 'White House,' and see the mules walk around, and the corn growing." His childhood was passed amid the stirring events of the second war with England. A British fleet under Admiral Cockburn ravaged the shores of the Chesapeake Bay and its large rivers, and on the 29th of August, 1814, the town of Alexandria, then his home, was captured by the enemy's vessels, and soon afterwards the opposite shore of the Potomac, and the city of Washington, were occupied by the enemy. These events occurring immediately under his eye when so young, may have had some effect in moulding his naturally gentle nature, and in giving the preference for the army. When he was eleven years old his father died. Then, his older brother being absent and his sisters very young, he became the stay and comfort of his pious and devoted mother.

Mrs. Lee remained in Alexandria, and was a communicant of "Christ Church." Her children were taught the Episcopal Catechism by the Rev. Wm. Meade, rector of the church, and afterwards the venerated Bishop of Virginia. Many years afterwards, when General Lee commanded the Army of Northern Virginia, he passed through Richmond, and hearing that the revered teacher and pastor of his boyhood was on his dying bed, at the house of a friend in that city, he immediately went to see him. When his name was mentioned to the Bishop, and a doubt expressed of the propriety of his seeing him in his weak state, he said, faintly:

"I must see him, if but for a few moments."

General Lee approached the bed evincing deep emotion, and, taking the emaciated hand, said to him:

"How are you to-day, Bishop?"

"Almost gone," replied Bishop Meade, in a voice scarcely audible; "but I wanted to see you once more. God bless you, Robert! God bless you, and fit you for your high and responsible duties. I can't call you General; I must call you Robert. I have heard your Catechism so often."

A brief conversation then ensued, the Bishop putting some pertinent questions to General Lee about the state of the country and the army, showing, as he always did, the most lively interest in the success of the Southern cause. It now seemed necessary to close the interview, such was the Bishop's exhaustion, but he pressed warmly the General's hand, saying, "Heaven bless you! Heaven bless you, end give you wisdom for your important and arduous duties." He could say no more. General Lee returned the pressure of the feeble hand, stood motionless by the bedside in perfect silence for some minutes, and then left the room. Bishop Meade died the next morning.

Alexandria continued to be the residence of his mother, and his devotion to her, invalid as she was, seems to have been one of the distinguishing traits of his boyhood. There are persons still living who remember how cheerfully he executed her orders and attended to her business, and how tenderly and untiringly he labored to promote her happiness. His self-denying devotion to her when a boy of eleven is often spoken of by a relative who was often with her at that time. His oldest brother, Carter, was then at Cambridge, Sidney Smith in the navy, one sister under the care of the physicians in Philadelphia, and the other too young for household cares; so that Robert was the housekeeper, carried the keys, attended to marketing, the horses, or anything which relieved the mind or lightened the burden of his sick and widowed mother. When school-hours were over, and other boys went to the play-ground, he would be seen running to assist his mother to be ready for her drive. The relative alluded to was often the companion of those drives, and remembers his efforts to amuse her, saying, with the gravity of a man, that unless she was cheerful the drive would not be beneficial; and if she complained of the draughts of air, he world pull out his knife and a newspaper, and amuse her by his efforts to improvise curtains, to protect her from the wind which whistled through the crevices of the old family-coach. When, at eighteen years of age, it became necessary for him to choose a profession, he chose the army, and obtained an appointment from Virginia as cadet at West Point. Then came the trial of parting with his mother, knowing, as he did, how sorrowful it would make her to give him up. "How can I live without Robert?" she was heard to say; "he is both son and daughter to me."

He entered the Military Academy in 1825, carrying with him the steady Christian character, and the determination to do right, which so signally marked his public and private course through life. He had been early taught, by his good mother and faithful pastor, his duty towards God and his neighbor, to "submit himself to all his governors and teachers, and to order himself lowly and reverently to all his betters;" therefore he found it comparatively easy to submit to the rigid discipline of the Institution. He left it in 1829, having passed through the whole course of four years without receiving a single demerit or being once reprimanded. He was noted for his studious habits and exemplary conduct. He never used an oath, drank intoxicating liquors, placed cards, or indulged in any of those bad practices so fatal to students, but unfortunately regarded by so many of them as marks of manliness or as mere sources of amusement, and the more enjoyed because forbidden. He never used tobacco in any shape.

On the 4th of July, 1829, he graduated first in his class, and received the appointment of Brevet Second Lieutenant in the Corps of Topographical Engineers, to which branch of the service the most distinguished graduates of West Point are assigned. Very soon after graduation, he was summoned to attend the dying bed of the mother whom he loved so much. She was ill at Ravensworth, the residence of the Hon. Wm. H. Fitzhugh, near Alexandria. Having obtained his furlough, he hastened thither, and nursed her with the tenderness and fidelity of a devoted daughter; administering her nourishment and medicine with his own hands, and rarely leaving her bedside until the distressing scene was over. One who knew him best says that it was from his good mother that he learned at an early age to "practise self-denial and self-control, as well as the strictest economy in all financial concerns," virtues which he retained and exercised throughout his checkered life. He was wont to say that he "owed everything to his mother."

When but a child, while his father was in the West Indies, during his last illness, he wrote to his son Carter, then a student at Cambridge, and speaking feelingly of his children, whom he was destined never to see again, he says:

Robert, who was always good, will be confirmed in his happy turn of mind by his ever watchful and affectionate mother.

This tender remark, which seems to have been written in the spirit of prophecy, shows how beautifully the boy, even at that early age, had fulfilled the commandment, "Honor thy father and thy mother," to both parents. To the teachers of his childhood, as well as to his schoolmates, his memory seems to be dear, as that of one who only gave them pleasure. They remember that Robert Lee was always regarded with love and respect by the whole school, and that he was remarkable for his quiet and peaceable disposition. His first teacher was a Mr. Leary, an Irish gentleman, who, twice after the war, went a great distance to see him, which meetings were greatly enjoyed by both teacher and pupil. He was taught mathematics by Mr. Benjamin Hallowell, a famous teacher in Alexandria, who still lives to give by letter the estimation in which he held his pupil, as the following extract will show:

Robert E. Lee entered my school in Alexandria, in the winter of 1824–25, to study mathematics preparatory to his going to West Point. He was a most exemplary student in every respect. He was never behind time at his studies; never failed in a single recitation; was perfectly observant of the rules and regulations of the Institution; was gentlemanly, unobtrusive, and respectful in all his deportment to teachers and to his fellow-students.

His specialty was finishing up. He imparted a finish and a neatness, as he proceeded, to everything he undertook. One of the branches of mathematics he studied with me was Conic Sections, in which some of the diagrams are very complicated. He drew the diagrams on a slate; and although he well knew that the one he was drawing would have to be removed to make room for another, he drew each one with as much accuracy and finish, lettering and all, as if it was to be engraved and printed. He carried the same traits be exhibited in my school to West Point, where I have been told he never received a demerit mark, and graduated head of his class.

A feeling of mutual kindness and respect continued between us to the close of his life. He was a great friend and advocate of education.

Mr. Hallowell, who was a Union man during the war, adds, "It was a matter of great regret to me that he thought it right to take the course he did in our recent national difficulties; but I never entertained a doubt that he was influenced by what he believed to be his duty, and what was entirely in harmony with the requirements of a gentleman and the dictates of honor.

CHAPTER III.BEGINNING OF HIS MILITARY CAREER.

AFTER this brief furlough and sad visit to his home, Lieutenant Lee entered upon the duties of his profession with the zeal and interest which foreshadowed success. In the spring of 1831 he was married, at Arlington, to Mary Randolph Custis, only child of George Washington Parke Custis, and granddaughter of the wife of General Washington. The marriage ceremony was performed by the Rev. Dr. Keith, of the Theological Seminary, near Alexandria.

After his marriage, Lieutenant Lee became, when on furlough, the resident of Arlington House, the beautiful home of his father-in-law. Soon afterwards he was sent to Fortress Monroe, Virginia, where he remained three years. In 1835 he was appointed Assistant Astronomer for marking out the boundary between Ohio and Michigan. In Sept., 1836, he was promoted to the rank of First Lieutenant, and in 1838 to a Captaincy. In 1838–39 he was sent to improve the navigation of the Mississippi at St. Louis, and to open a passage for the river at Des Moines Rapids. While absent from home, and working so skilfully for his country, his warm heart longed for the dear ones from whom he was necessarily so much separated. "His care and anxiety for his children,–writes one who knew him best, "commenced with the first; and though he was so frequently absent from them, their obedience to his commands was perfect, as was their respect for his wishes; and certainly his example never misled them."

In a letter written to his wife, when far from home, and while his children were very young, we find this extract:

The improved condition of the children, which you mention, was a source of great comfort to me; and as I suppose, by this time, you have all returned to Arlington, you will be able to put them under a proper restraint, which you were probably obliged to relax while visiting among strangers, and which that indulgence will now render more essential. Our dear little boy seems to have among his friends the reputation of being hard to manage,—a distinction not at all desirable, as it indicates self-will and obstinacy. Perhaps these are qualities which he really possesses, arid he may have a better right to them than I am willing to acknowledge; but it is our duty, if possible, to counteract them, and assist him to bring them under his control. I have endeavored, in my intercourse with him, to require nothing but what was in my opinion necessary or proper, and to explain to him temperately its propriety, at a time when he could listen to my arguments, and not at the moment of his being vexed, and his little faculties warped by passion. I have also tried to show him that I was firm in my demands and constant in their enforcement, and that he must comply with them; and I let him see that I looked to their execution in order to relieve him, as much as possible, from the temptation to break them. Since my efforts have been so unsuccessful, I fear I have altogether failed in accomplishing my purpose, but I hope to be able to profit by my experience. You must assist me in my attempts, and we must endeavor to combine the mildness and forbearance of the mother with the sternness and, perhaps, unreasonableness of the father. This is a subject on which I think much, though M— may blame me for not reading more. I am ready to acknowledge the good advice contained in the text-books, and believe that I see the merit of their reasoning generally; but what I want to learn is, to apply what I already know. I pray God to watch over, and direct our efforts in guarding our dear little son, that we may bring him up in the way he should go. . . .

. . . Oh what pleasure I lose in being separated from my children. Nothing can compensate me for that; still I must remain here, ready to perform what little service I can, and hope for the best.

This letter is dated St. Louis, Oct. 16th, 1837.

This extract, showing his wisdom and love in endeavoring to train so young a child, seems too good to be withheld from parents, for their instruction and example. Another letter, showing how tender and amiable he was in his domestic relations, was written nearly two years afterwards, while still on duty in the West.

LOUISVILLE, June 5th, 1839.

MY DEAREST MARY:—I arrived here last night, and before going out this morning I will inform you of my well-doing thus far.

After leaving Staunton, I got on very well, but did not reach Guyandotte till Sunday evening, where, before alighting from the stage, I espied a boat descending the river, in which I took passage to Cincinnati. . . .

. . . You do not know how much I have missed you and the children, my dear Mary. To be alone in a crowd is very solitary. In the woods I feel sympathy with the trees and birds in whose company I take delight, but experience no interest in a strange crowd. I hope you are till well, and will continue so; and therefore must again urge upon you to be very prudent and careful of those dear children. If I could only get a squeeze at that little fellow turning up his sweet mouth to "keese Baba!" You must not let him run wild in my absence, and will have to exercise firm authority over all of them. This will not require seventy, or even strictness, but constant attention, and an unwavering course. Mildness and forbearance, tempered by firmness and judgment, will strengthen their affection for you, while it will maintain your control over them.

In 1842 Captain Lee was sent to Fort Hamilton, in New York harbor, and while there was, in 1844, appointed a member of the board of visitors at West Point. In 1845 he was a member of the board of Engineers, and in 1846, when the Mexican War broke out, he was assigned to the duty of Chief Engineer of the Central Army of Mexico, in which capacity he served with great ability to the end of the war.

While still at Fort Hamilton, the following letter was written to one of his sons:

FORT HAMILTON, March 31st, 1846.

I cannot go to bed, my dear son, without writing you a few lines to thank you for your letter, which gave me great pleasure. I am glad to hear you are well, and hope you are learning to read and write, and that the next letter you will be able to write yourself. I want to see you very much, and to tell you all that has happened since you went away. I do not think I ever told you of a fine boy I heard of in my travels this winter. He lived in the mountains of New Hampshire. He was just thirteen years old, the age of Custis. His father was a farmer, and he used to assist him to work on his farm as much as he could. The snow there this winter was deeper than it has been for years, and one day he accompanied his father into the woods to get some wood. They went with their wood-sled, and after cutting a load and loading the sled, this little boy, whose name was Harry, drove it home, while his father cut another load. He had a fine team of horses, and returned very quickly, when he found his father lying prostrate on the frozen snow, under the limb of a large tree he had felled during his absence, which had caught him in its fall and thrown him to the ground. He was cold and stiff; and little Harry finding he was not strong enough to relieve him from his position, seized his axe and cut off the limb, and rolled it off of him. He then tried to raise him, but his father was dead, and his feeble efforts were in vain. Although he was far out in the woods by himself, and had never before seen a dead person, he was nothing daunted, but backed the sled close up to his father, and with great labor got his body on it, and placing his head in his lap, drove home to his mother as fast as he could. The efforts of his mother to reanimate him were equally vain with his own, and the sorrowing neighbors came and dug him a grave under the cold snow, and laid him to rest. His mother was greatly distressed at the loss of her husband, but she thanked God, who had given her so good and brave a son.

You and Custis must take great care of your kind mother and dear sisters, when your father is dead. To do that, you must learn to be good. Be true, kind, and generous, and pray earnestly to God to enable you to "keep his commandments, and walk in the same all the days of your life." Alec and Frank are well, and the former has begun to ride his pony Jim again. Captain Bennett has bought his little boy a donkey, and as I came home I met him riding, with two large Newfoundland dogs following, one on each side. The dogs were almost as large as the donkey. My horse, Jerry, did not know what to make of them. I go to New York now, on horseback, every day; one day I ride Jerry, and the next Tom, and I think they begin to go better under the saddle than formerly. I hope to come on soon, to see that little baby you have got to show me. You must give her a kiss for me, and one to all the children, and to your mother and grandmother. Good-bye, my dear son.

Your affectionate father, R. E. LEE.

CHAPTER IV. MEXICAN WAR.

THE time had now come for Captain Lee to change the quiet of garrison life for the stirring scenes of war. Hostilities now commenced with Mexico. General Scott began early in 1847 to collect troops on the island of Lobos, for an expedition against Vera Cruz. Captain Lee had been assigned to the central army of Mexico, and was now Chief Engineer under General Wool.

The following letter to his sons, Custis and W. H. F. Lee, was written about this time.

SHIP MASSACHUSETTS, OFF LOBOS,

Feb. 27th, 1847.

MY DEAR BOYS:—I received your letters with the greatest pleasure, and, as I always like to talk to you both together, I will not separate you in my letters, but write one to both. I was much gratified to hear of your progress at school, and hope you will continue to advance, and that I shall have the happiness of finding you much improved in your studies, on my return. I shall not feel my long separation from you, if I find that my absence has been of no injury to you, and that you have both grown in goodness and knowledge as well as in stature. But ah, how much I will suffer on my return, if I find the reverse has occurred! You enter into all my thoughts, in all my prayers; and on you, in part, will depend whether I shall be happy or miserable, as you know how much I love you. You must do all in your power to save me pain. You will learn, by my letter to your grandmother, that I have been to Tampico. I saw many things to remind me of you, though that was not necessary to make me wish that you were with me. The river was so calm and beautiful, and the boys were playing about in boats, and swimming their ponies. Then there were troops of donkeys carrying water through the streets. They had a kind of saddle, something like a cart-saddle, though larger, that carried two ten-gallon kegs on each side, which was a load for a donkey. They had no bridles on, but would come along in strings to the river, and, as soon as their kegs were filled, start off again. They were fatter and sleeker than any donkeys I had ever seen before, and seemed to be better cared for. I saw a great many ponies, too. They were larger than those in the upper country, but did not seem so enduring. I got one to ride around the fortifications. He had a Mexican bit and saddle on, and paced delightfully, but every time my sword struck him on the flanks, he would jump, and try to run off. Several of them had been broken to harness by the Americans, and I saw some teams ill wagons, driven four-in-hand, well matched, and trotting well. We had a grand parade on General Scott's arrival. The troops were all drawn up on the bank of the river, and fired a salute as he passed them. He landed at the market, where lines of sentinels were placed to keep off the crowd. In front of the landing the artillery was drawn up, which received him in the centre of the column and escorted him through the streets to his lodgings. They had provided a handsome gray horse, richly caparisoned for him to ride, but he preferred to walk with his staff around him, and a dragoon led the horse behind us. The windows along the streets we passed were crowded with people, and the boys and girls were in great glee. The Governor's Island band played all the time.

There were six thousand soldiers in Tampico. Mr. Barry was the Adjutant of the escort. I think you would have enjoyed with me the oranges and sweet potatoes. Major Smith became so fond of the coffee, that I could hardly get him away from the house. We only remained there one day. I have a nice state-room on board this ship. Joe Johnston and myself occupy it, but my poor Joe is so sick all the time, I can do nothing with him. I left Jem to come on with the horses, as I was afraid they would not be properly cared for. Vessels were expressly fitted up for the horses, and parties of dragoons detailed to take care of them. I had hoped they would reach here by this time, as I wanted to see how they were fixed. I took every precaution for their comfort, provided them with bran, oats, etc., and had slings made to pass under them and attach the coverings above, so that, if in the heavy sea they should slip, or be thrown off their feet, they should not fall. I had to sell my good old horse "Jem," as I could not find room for him, or, rather, I did not want to crowd the others. I know I shall want him when I land. Creole was the admiration of every one at Brazos, and they could hardly believe she had carried me so far and looked so well. Jem says there is nothing like her in all the country, and I believe he likes her better than Tom or Jerry. The sorrel mare did not appear to be so well after I got to the Brazos. I had put one of the men on her whose horse had given out, and the saddle hurt her back. She had gotten well, however, before I left, and I told Jem to ride her every day. I hope they may both reach the shore in safety, but I fear they will have a hard time. They will have to be put on board a steamboat and carried to the ship that lies about two miles out at sea, then hoisted in, and hew we shall get them on shore again I do not know. Probably throw them overboard, and let them swim there. I do not think we shall remain here more than one day longer. General Worth's and General Twiggs's divisions have arrived, which include the regulars, and I suppose the volunteers will be coming on every day. . . .

. . . Tell Rob he must think of me very often, be a good boy, and always love his papa. Take care of Speck* and the colts. Mr. Sedgwick and all the officers send their love to you. The ship rolls so that I can scarcely write. You must write to me very often. I am always glad to hear from you. Be sure that I am thinking of you, and that you have the prayers of

Your affectionate father,

R. E. LEE.

The skill of Captain Lee as an engineer had impressed the military authorities most favorably, and particularly General Winfield Scott; and during the Mexican war he was entrusted with the most difficult enterprises. At the siege of Vera Cruz he rendered important services, and General Scott appointed him to a position on his personal staff, and always asked and attached great importance to his opinion in council. "I am compelled," says General Scott, in his Autobiography, "to make special mention of Captain R. E. Lee, Engineer. This officer greatly distinguished himself at the siege of Vera Cruz." Indeed, his whole career in Mexico was most distinguished; and his veteran commander mentioned him honorably in almost every dispatch. In making a reconnoissance from Cerro Gordo, Captain Lee ventured so far from his column, that he found himself in the midst of the enemy. He concealed himself under a fallen tree, near a spring where the Mexicans obtained water. The Mexicans passed and repassed over the tree, and even sat upon it, without discovering him. He remained there until night enabled him to make his escape. On one occasion, u hen the two advanced divisions of the Mexican army lay in the valley of the Plan-de-Rio, and the body of the army, about three miles off, on the heights of Cerro Gordo, it became necessary, to success, that a road should be opened for batteries on the mountains in the rear of the enemy: the difficult task was allotted to Captain Lee, at the head of a body of pioneers. At the end of three days the way was opened, and a light battery put in position, to the dismay of the Mexican General Santa Anna, who said that he had not believed that a goat could approach him in that direction. Hence the surprise to the Mexicans, and great results.

General William Preston, who knew him first in Mexico, said of him, "He was a man of great personal beauty and grace of body. . . . . There were discerning minds that appreciated his genius, and saw in him the coming Captain of America. He belonged to a club which was then organized, together with General McClellan, General Albert Sydney Johnston, General Beauregard, and a host of others, who recognized Lee as a master-spirit. He never swore an oath; he never drank; he was never violent; he never wrangled. He was averse to quarrelling, and not a single difficulty marked his career; but all acknowledged his justness and wonderful evenness of mind. Rare intelligence, combined with these qualities, served to make him a fit representative of his great prototype—General Washington." "He came from Mexico," says President Davis, in his address delivered at Richmond, Va., after the death of General Lee, "crowned with honors, covered by brevets, and recognized, young as he was, as one of the ablest of his country's soldiers. And to prove that he was estimated then as such, let me tell you that when Lee was a captain of engineers, stationed in Baltimore, the Cuban Junta in New York selected him to be their leader in the struggle for the independence of their native country. They were anxious to secure his services, and offered him every temptation that ambition could desire. He thought the matter over, and, I remember, came to Washington to consult me as to what he should do; and when I began to discuss the complications which might arise from his acceptance of the trust, he gently rebuked me, saying that this was not the line upon which he wished my advice: the simple was, 'Whether it was right or not?'" Such was his determination to do right, that the most tempting offers of ambition or wealth could not make him diverge one iota from the path of duty. After lauding his military genius, Mr. Davis says: "His moral qualities rose to the height of his genius. Self-denying; always intent upon the one idea of duty; self-controlled to an extent that many thought him cold. His feelings were really warm, and his heart melted freely at the sight of a wounded soldier, or the story of the sufferings of the widow and orphan."

Notes

* A little dog.

CHAPTER V. HE RETURNS HOME ON A FURLOUGH AND JOINS THE CHURCH.

IT was in the summer of 1853, in old Christ Church, Alexandria, during one of his visits to his family at Arlington, that he renewed his baptismal covenant, and openly enlisted under the banner of the Cross, engaging to "continue Christ's faithful servant and soldier unto his life's end." It was in that old church, picturesque in its antique beauty, ivy-covered, and surrounded by trees the growth of more than a century—the church where Washington worshipped from week to week, after his retirement to Mount Vernon, and whose square pew is now kept just as he left it, the association never having been destroyed by the desecrating hand of "modern improvement,"—in that church in which his sainted mother worshipped, in which he had been taught the Catechism by Bishop Meade, and trained to "Remember his Creator in the days his youth," that Colonel Robert E. Lee was confirmed by Bishop Johns. He approached the chancel with a daughter on each arm, who knelt with their father for the same holy purpose. He was then in his forty-sixth year. From his childhood, the desire of his life seems to have been to do right. His unselfish devotion to his mother; his course at West Point, in which he seems to have kept himself unspotted from the world; his almost blameless course in the army and in domestic life, would seem to indicate that the early seed of religion, so earnestly sown, had taken deep root, and that the motives of his conduct were purified by Divine grace. Of his reasons for not being earlier a professed Christian, we know nothing; we only know that now, while quietly resting from the active duties of his soldier's life, he felt that he must, as a Christian, confess Christ before men; and there never was to his dying day a "sliding in his steps."

We cannot follow him through his rapid promotion in the army. After having been three years in the honorable post of Superintendent of the United States Military Academy, West Point, we find him, in 1855, commissioned Lieutenant-Colonel, in full rank, of the Second Regiment of Cavalry. The Colonel of that regiment was the lamented Albert Sydney Johnston, afterwards General in the Confederate service, who fell, in the zenith of his fame, on the field of Shiloh. In that year (1855) he was sent to Texas, and was often actively engaged in Indian warfare, and remained there till his recall at the breaking out of the Civil War in 1861.

In 1859 Colonel Lee returned to Arlington on furlough, and while there he was called away from his family to take part in what is known as the "John Brown raid." On the night of the 16th of October, a band of conspirators, led by a desperado named John Brown, who had been notorious in the North-West territories as an offender against the laws, attacked Harper's Ferry, for the purpose of taking possession of the United States Armory, which contained about fifty thousand small arms. The avowed purpose was to arm the slaves of the State, and to incite them to insurrection. Several citizens were fired on and killed, and others taken prisoners. The news of the outbreak was at once telegraphed to Washington, and the militia of the surrounding country were ordered out, to put down the insurrection. President Buchanan dispatched a battalion of marines, under the command of Colonel Lee, to arrest the rioters. Brow and his men had retreated to the engine-house, and fortified it. They had with them a number of the prisoners. This house Colonel Lee immediately on his arrival surrounded, to prevent the escape of Brown, but deferred the attack until next morning, lest the captive citizens might be injured. At daylight on the 18th, Colonel Lee sent his aid, Lieutenant J. E. B. Stuart, to demand the surrender of the insurgents, promising to protect them from the violence of the citizens. Brown refused. Finding that nothing but force could avail, Colonel Lee ordered the attack; and the marines by a gallant assault captured the building and its inmates, several of whom were killed or wounded. Brown was among the latter. The marines lost one man killed, and one wounded; but providentially none of the citizens captured by Brown were injured. Colonel Lee protected his prisoners from the enraged citizens, until orders were received from Washington to turn them over to the Virginia authorities; and having performed the duty assigned him, he returned to Washington. At the expiration of his furlough he joined his regiment in Texas, where he remained until he was recalled to Washington, in 1861.

CHAPTER VI. BEGINNING OF THE CIVIL WAR.

OF the causes of this war, it is not proper in this little volume to speak. That it became necessary must ever be a source of regret to both sections of the country. When Lee returned to Washington, he found the whole country burning with passions which betokened war. South Carolina had seceded, and was soon followed by the States bordering on the Gulf of Mexico. Early in February a government was formed at Montgomery, in Alabama, and the Hon. Jefferson Davis, of Mississippi, was elected President of the Confederate States. Virginia for some time clung to the Union, which she revered. She could not see it dismembered without an effort for peace. She looked on with sorrow, and could not see her sister States, so long united, tearing themselves apart without interposing to heal the wounds and reunite them. She cried aloud for peace! peace! but it was all in vain. The peace convention at Washington, from which she hoped so much, had failed to promote harmony. The President of the United States had demanded seventy-five thousand men to "put down the rebellion," of which Virginia was to give her quota to force her sisters of the South into obedience to Federal authority. She must at once decide on her own course, and she did decide to leave the Federal Union, and having decided according to her thorough conviction of right, she did it by an overwhelming vote, and threw her whole influence on the Southern side. And now she stood ready to bare her breast to the impending storm which must sweep over and desolate her from the Potomac to the Roanoke—from Chesapeake Bay to the Ohio and Big Sandy rivers. Her sons were ready at the tap of the drum to rush to her defence, and her daughters, with scarcely less patriotism, at once came forward to take their parts in the great trials that awaited them. None but those who witnessed the efforts made by the Southern women in every State of the Confederacy, can realize all that was done and suffered by them in behalf of a cause which seemed to them so just and righteous. In every city, town, village or country neighborhood, they met together in societies with but one object in view—to aid the soldiers. Fair and delicate hands from the highest walks of life were engaged in cutting and sewing the coarsest clothing, knitting socks, and scraping lint for wounds not yet made. Self-denial was added to industry; delicacies were given up; extravagance of dress, and luxurious ease were abandoned. Throughout the four years they never ceased their efforts. The battles being fought, the hospitals demanded their attention—binding up the wounds, soothing the sick, comforting the distressed, praying with the dying, became their mission; and nobly did they fulfil it. The mothers of Sparta, the matrons of Rome, the Florence Nightingales of England, all belonged to the morally sublime; but no women could have excelled the mothers, the wives, the daughters and sisters of our lamented Southern Confederacy. The South was, as it were, walled around by the blockade. She must depend on herself. Alone and unaided by the outside world, nothing was left to her but her own strength, and her calm reliance on the mercy and justice of God. While her daughters buckled on the armor of those dearer to them than life itself, they did it with firm hands and prayerful hearts; and though the unbidden tear might start, the encouraging word and cheering smile were freely given, The loved ones would depart with a cheerful and heartfelt "God bless you" ringing in their ears, while the blanched lips which uttered it would in another moment be pouring out for them in secret the "cry of faith to the ear of mercy."

Virginia being fairly out of the Union, Robert E. Lee, now in Washington, had a solemn question to decide, and one which stirred up the purest and deepest feelings of his great heart. Must he resign, and give up the flag under which he had been born and educated, had fought and bled, and under which he had gained laurels which could never wither? Must he leave his old comrades in arms, and his old commander General Scott, and fight against them? Or must he draw his sword against his mother, Virginia, against his home and kindred? The decision with most men would have been difficult—doubts and fears would have disturbed them, but with him the governing motive of his life came to his aid. He must do right, and on this great occasion he knew the right, and unhesitatingly pursued it. Every argument which General Scott could offer was powerless to shake his resolution to resign. In answer to his urgent appeals, he replied, "I am compelled to do it. I cannot consult my feelings in this matter." "My husband," wrote Mrs. Lee to a friend, about this time, "has wept tears of blood over this terrible war; but he must, as a man and as a Virginian, share the destiny of his State, which has solemnly pronounced for independence." Accordingly, he wrote from Arlington, on the 20th of April, 1861, the following letter to General Scott, enclosing his resignation:

ARLINGTON, VA., April 20th, 1861.

GENERAL:—Since my interview with you on the 18th instant, I have felt that I ought not longer to retain my commission in the army. I therefore tender my resignation, which I request that you will recommend for acceptance. It would have been presented at once, but for the struggle it has cost me to separate myself from a service to which I have devoted the best years of my life, and all the ability I possessed. During the whole of that time—more than a quarter of a century—I have experienced nothing but kindness from my superiors, and the most cordial friendship from my comrades. To no one, General, have I been as much indebted as to yourself for uniform kindness and consideration; and it has always been m y ardent desire to merit your approbation. I shall carry to my grave the most grateful recollections of your kind consideration; and your name and fame will always be dear to me. Save in defence of my native State, I never desire again to draw my sword. Be pleased to accept my most earnest wishes for the continuance of your happiness and prosperity, and believe me,

Most truly yours,

R. E. LEE.

Lieutenant-General WINFIELD SCOTT,

Commanding United States Army.

In an affectionate letter written the same day to a sister, who, with her husband, remained in the Union, he says:

I know that you will blame me; but you must think of me as kindly as you can, and believe that I have endeavored to do what I thought right.

CHAPTER VII. LEE GOES TO VIRGINIA, AND IS MADE COMMANDER OF HER FORCES.

HAD General Lee been ambitious, he would have remained in the Union. He was regarded by the whole Federal Government, as well as General Scott, as the most promising officer in the army. General Preston, in the speech already quoted, says he remembered when General Scott used these remarkable words: "I tell you one thing, if I were on my dying bed, and knew there was to be a battle fought for the liberties of my country, and the President was to say to me, 'Scott, who shall command?' I tell you, that with my dying breath I should say, Robert E. Lee; nobody but Robert lee, Robert Lee, and nobody but Lee." Therefore, it is certain that the highest military honors awaited him. It is believed that the President offered him the command of the whole Union army. He also knew that in going South, he was going into a great military struggle which seemed hopeless—and that he must give wealth for poverty, and be proclaimed a traitor to the world by the Government which had been so dear to him.

Arlington, too, the beautiful home of his family, must be left in the hands of the enemy. We have seen it in its wonderful, picturesque beauty, with its sloping lawns, its grand old oaks and maples, its noble portico, from which we enjoyed the view of the blue Potomac, with the cities of Washington and Georgetown laid out before it, Adorning its ample halls were innumerable relics brought from Mount Vernon by the father of Mrs. Lee, the adopted son of Washington. Here were to be found the original portraits of General and Mrs. Washington, painted about the time of their marriage. Here also was the original portrait of General Washington, painted by Sharpless, a distinguished English artist who painted in crayons. Many other pictures, and several pieces of the old furniture from Mount Vernon were there; the candelabra which had given it light; the tea-table at which Mrs. Washington had always presided. The china presented to Mrs. Washington by certain English merchants, on which was her monogram; that given to Genera Washington by the Society of the Cincinnati; a book-case made by General Washington's own direction; and above all, the bedstead, bed, and pillows on which the Father of his country breathed out his precious life—all these and far more were left to the uncertain future.

Mrs. Lee and her daughters were soon obliged to follow him, and take refuge in the interior of Virginia, among friends, until another home could be provided for them. His two sons, who were officers in the army, like their noble father, soon resigned, to cast their lot in with the young Confederacy; while his younger son, a mere youth, went, with so many of the first young men of the country, into the ranks of the Southern army.

As soon as the news of Lee's resignation reached Richmond, Governor Letcher conferred on him the rank of Major-General, and the command of the Virginia forces, as authorized by the Virginia Legislature. This appointment was not solicited by Colonel Lee; but he did not feel at liberty to decline it. It was confirmed by the Convention, and the decision of that body was communicated to him on the 23d of April by John Janney, its President.

General Lee stood in the middle aisle of the legislative hall of he capitol, and the president thus addressed him:

MAJOR-GENERAL LEE:—In the name of the people of your native State, here represented, I bid you a cordial and heartfelt welcome to this hall, in which we may almost yet hear the echo of the voices of the statesmen, the soldiers, and sages of by-gone days, who have borne your name, and whose blood now flows in p a r veins. . . .

When the necessity became apparent of having a leader for our forces, all hearts and eyes, by the impulse of an instinct, which is a surer guide than reason itself, turned to the old county of Westmoreland. We knew how prolific she had been in other days of heroes and statesmen. We knew she had given birth to the Father of his country, to Richard Henry Lee, to Monroe, and last, though not least, to your own gallant father; and we knew well, by your deeds, that her productive power was not yet exhausted. . . .

Sir, one of the proudest recollections of my life will be the honor that I yesterday had of submitting to this body the confirmation of the nomination, made by the Governor of this State, of you as Commander-in-Chief of the military and naval forces of this Commonwealth. I rose to put the question; and when I asked if this body would advise and consent to that appointment, there rushed from the hearts to the tongues of all the members an affirmative response, which told, with an emphasis that could leave no doubt, of the feeling whence it emanated, I put the negative of the question for form's sake, but there was an unbroken silence.

Sir, we have, by this unanimous vote, expressed our convictions that you are at this day, among the living citizens of Virginia, "first in war." We pray God most fervently that you may so conduct the operations committed to your charge that it may soon be said of you that you are "first in peace;" and when the time comes, you will have earned the still prouder distinction of being "first in the hearts of your countrymen."

I will close with one more remark. When the Father of his country made his last will and testament, he gave swords to his favorite nephews, with an injunction that they should never be drawn from their scabbards except in self-defence, or in defence of the rights and liberties of their country; and that if drawn for the latter purpose, they should fall with them in their hands, rather than relinquish them.

Yesterday, your mother, Virginia, placed her sword in your hand, upon the implied condition, that we know you will keep to the letter and in spirit, that you will draw it only in her defence, and that you will fall with it in your hand rather than the object for which it was placed there shall fail.

To this address, General Lee replied:

MR. PRESIDENT AND GENTLEMEN OF THE CONVENTION:—Profoundly impressed with the solemnity of the occasion, for which I must say I was not prepared, I accept the position assigned me by your partiality. I would have much preferred your choice had fallen upon an abler man. Trusting in Almighty God, an approving conscience, and the aid of my fellow-citizens, I devote myself to the service of my native State, in whose behalf alone will I ever again draw my sword.

General Lee at once began the task of organizing the State forces, and putting the country in a state of defence. The duty was performed within a short time, and with great success. On the 6th of May, Virginia became a member of the Confederate States, and transferred her forces to the Government; and on the 10th, General Lee was ordered by the President to retain the command of the Virginia forces until the military organization of the Confederacy was placed on a firm basis. In July, 1861, he was made a General in the army of the Confederate States. General Lee, with characteristic modesty, sought no notoriety, but was always contented to do his duty in the situation in which he was placed. At a later period of the war he uttered the sentiment which always influenced him, when he said, "I will take any position the country assigns to me, and do the best I can."

When the war commenced in April, 1861, Lee was fifty-three years old, in the full vigor of his manhood. His figure was erect, with the military air of the professed soldier, derived from his West Point education and service in the army. We well remember the grave dignity of his elegant deportment, increased tenfold afterwards by high command and great responsibilities. He had always been remarkable for manly beauty of face and figure, which was now particularly striking, before time had implanted wrinkles, or care gray hairs; his moustache was dark and heavy; he then wore no beard; and his fresh color was indicative of robust health. His habits were now as they ever were, temperate in all things, rarely drinking so much as a single glass of wine; and his indifference about what he ate became notorious in the army. His abstaining from the "soldier's comfort," smoking and chewing, throughout the war, was a matter of intense surprise to the men. He seemed now, as at West Point and in Mexico, superior to those habits to which the soldier is so prone. The truth and frankness of his character, his warm heart, generosity and honesty, were wonderfully expressed in his fine open countenance and simple, unassuming manners. Such was General Lee in person and manner in the beginning of the war. He seemed then a man of great reserve; he was quiet and thoughtful. His mind was evidently full of the responsibilities of his position. How could it have been otherwise? He did not enter upon it lightly, but in the fear of God; he had undertaken a great work, and with God alone for his guide, he must pursue it with diligence and gravity. The truth and honesty of his character seem well expressed in a letter to his eldest son, written many years ago, but which every boy and girl in this country should study until the sentiments expressed become engrafted upon their very natures:

"You must study," he wrote, "to be frank with the world; frankness is the child of honesty and courage. Say just what you mean to do on every occasion, and take it for granted you mean to do right. If a friend ask a favor, you should grant it, if it is reasonable; if not, tell him plainly why you cannot. You will wrong him and wrong yourself by equivocation of any kind. Never do wrong to make a friend or keep one; the man who requires you to do so is dearly purchased at a sacrifice. Deal kindly but firmly with all your classmates; you will find it the policy which wears best. Above all, do not appear to others what you are not. If you have any fault to find with any one, tell him, not others, of what you complain; there is no more dangerous experiment than that of undertaking to be one thing before a man's face and another behind his back. We should live, act, and say nothing to the injury of any one. It is not only best as a matter of principle, but it is the path to peace and honor.

"In regard to duty, let me, in conclusion of this hasty letter, inform you that nearly a hundred years ago there was a day of remarkable gloom and darkness—still known as 'the dark day,'—a day when the light of the sun was slowly extinguished as if by an eclipse. The Legislature of Connecticut was in session, and its members saw the unexpected and unaccountable darkness coming on. They shared in the general awe and terror. It was supposed by many that the last day had come. Some one, in the consternation of the hour, moved an adjournment. Then there arose an old Puritan legislator, Davenport, of Stamford, and said that if the last day had come, he desired to be found at his place doing his duty, and therefore moved that candles be brought in, so that the House could proceed with its duty. There was quietness in that man's mind, the quietness of heavenly wisdom and inflexible willingness to obey present duty. Duty, then, is the sublimest word in our language. Do your duty in all things, like the old Puritan, You cannot do more; you should never do less. Never let me and your mother wear one gray hair for any lack of duty on your part."

Such were the sentiments by which he wished his young son to be governed at school, and in his whole conduct during life such were the sentiments which governed the father; hence the greatness, the sublimity of his character; hence his calmness and resolution under his greatest difficulties; hence, when the cause for which he had given up all things, and which was so dear to him, failed; when his heart was near breaking for his country's sorrow, he stood calm and resigned in the midst of general disaster; for, like the old Puritan, he was in his place, doing his duty. He was a true Christian; his Christianity ennobled him, and made his path clear to him wherever he was, in whatever engaged. He ever felt that God watched over him, and would "make all things work together for good to those who loved him."

What other feeling would have given rise to that more than noble expression, "Human virtue should be equal to human calamity," when all was lost, and when the minds of other men seemed sinking under sorrow and disappointment. He knew that he had "done what he could," and God enabled him to bear the cruel defeat.

CHAPTER VIII. GENERAL LEE IN RICHMOND PUTTING IT IN A STATE OF DEFENCE.

THE war having fairly commenced, we must trace rapidly his progress. He was not on the field during the first few months of the war, but at his post in Richmond, using mighty efforts to put Virginia in a state of defence. He knew that from her geographical position, she must be the battle-field for immense armies. The Government called for troops, and the "raw material," men full of patriotism and valor, but without military training, poured into Richmond every day; training-camps were established, and officers who had had military educations appointed to drill them. In every town in the South, nothing was heard but the dill of military preparations; but Richmond, now the Confederate Capital, was the busiest point of all. The Federal Government threatened her. General Scott proposed taking his Fourth-of-July dinner there. The "On to Richmond" became the battle-cry of the Federal army, and therefore, to put the strategic points of the State, as well as the city, in a posture of defence, became his imperative duty. Volunteer regiments from the Gulf States, from Georgia, the Carolinas, and Virginia sprang up like magic. Tennessee and Arkansas contributed noble soldiers; and even Kentucky and Maryland, in despite of their governments, afforded regiments as valorous as any that ennobled the Confederate army—men of daring, who were obliged to leave their own borders by stealth to avoid arrest. But all these men mist be drilled, armed, and equipped; arms were few and ammunition scarce. It required great minds and indomitable energies to have these wants supplied. Workshops for the manufacture of arms and ammunition arose speedily, and in an incredibly short time Virginia was ready to receive the mighty demonstrations of the Federal Government.

General Lee was at the helm planning and organizing, and, when occasion arose, sending troops to the field; the strategic points were made strong, and three steamers were converted into vessels of war. Skirmishing was going on at various points, but the first engagement of any importance took place on the 10th of June, at Big Bethel, between Yorktown and Hampton, in which Colonel Magruder, by skill and strategy, signally defeated General Butler. This affair was small in itself, but very encouraging to the Confederates. Then followed the brief campaign of General Joe Johnston and Patterson in the Valley, in which the South was successful; but it was soon followed by the defeat of Colonel Pegram, and the death of the gallant General Robert Garnett during his retreat from Laurel Ridge. Then came the great battle of Manassas, involving, perhaps, the most signal defeat with which the Federals met during the war. Generals Beauregard and Joe Johnston there won laurels which can never fade; and there the revered General Jackson, then merely a Brigadier, was first called "Stonewall," because his brigade, always noted for its bravery, stood as immovable as a stone wall to receive the showers of shot and shell with which the enemy assailed it. "See," said the gallant General Bee, of Georgia, while encouraging his troops, "see, Jackson stands like a stone wall to repel the invaders." General Lee's place, then, was in Richmond, sending off reinforcements to the field, and completing those fortifications which elicited the admiration even of the Federal officers. "While the fortifications of Richmond stand," writes a Northern officer, "Lee will evoke admiration; the art of war is unacquainted with any defence so admirable."

General Lee was first sent to the field in the summer of 1861, to operate against "General Rosecrans in the mountains of Western Virginia. Soon after getting there, he found that the nature of the country, wild and mountainous in the extreme, and the hostility of many of the inhabitants to the Southern came, made it impossible to make an offensive movement."

"The movement against Cheat Mountain, which failed," wrote one of his officers, "was undertaken with the view of causing the enemy to contract his lines, and to enable us to reunite the troops of Generals Jackson, of Georgia, and Loring. After the failure of this movement on our part, General Rosecrans, feeling secure, strengthened his lines in that part of the country, and went with a part of his forces to the Kanawha, driving our forces across the Gauley. General Lee then went to that line of operations, to endeavor to unite the forces under Generals Floyd and Wise, and stop the movements under Rosecrans. General Loring, with a part of his force from Valley Mountain, joined the forces at Sewell Mountain. Rosecrans's movements were stopped, and the season for operations in that country being over, General Lee was ordered to Richmond, and soon after sent to South Carolina, to meet the movements of the enemy from "Port Royal," etc. His engineering skill in fortifying the coasts of South Carolina and Georgia was highly appreciated by the people of those States; and it was owing to the admirable construction of those defences, that the Federal efforts in that quarter afterwards met with so little success. They had already taken possession of Port Royal, and were threatening the interior."

General Lee was recalled to Richmond in the early spring of 1862, and on the 10th of March, duty was assigned him at the seat of Government, and under the direction of the President, he was charged with the conduct of the military operations of the Confederate armies. He was very popular in his new position; fresh life was at once infused into the Government, and the military situation at once seemed to grow brighter. His courtesy, and entire simplicity of manner, were now peculiarly apparent. Some persons seemed to expect him to make a great military display, and could scarcely realize that the plain, quiet gentleman who rode daily about the lines of Richmond, clad in simple gray, was "bending all the energies of a genius second to none in the world, to one of the most arduous tasks that ever tried the skill and patience of a soldier." He remained in this position a very short time; circumstances soon transpired which called him to the field, and the President, at his request, relieved him from the general control of all the armies. The moment had come when his generalship was to be tested by a command worthy of his great abilities. The largest and most important army was put under his control, and the defence of Richmond, the capital of the Confederacy.

His family, in the meantime had been living at the "White House," on the Pamunkey River. This fine estate had been the properly of Mrs. General Washington, the grandmother of Mrs. Lee, and was still owned by her immediate family. It was in this house, made so famous during the war by becoming a favorable "base" for the Federals, that Washington had wooed and won the fascinating Mrs. Custis; and it was either in this house, or in the neighborhood church, the venerable "St. Peter's," that afterwards married her. There Mrs. Lee and her young daughters took refuge, after it had become necessary for them to leave Arlington, vainly hoping to be safe from intrusion and danger. It was in June of 1862, when the Federal army was moving towards Richmond from the Peninsula, that she received intelligence that the enemy was approaching. She and her daughters immediately departed to the house of a friend, nearer Richmond, but not until she had affixed a paper to the door, imploring the Northern soldiers to forbear to desecrate the house in which Washington had spent the first part of his married life, and signed it, "A grand-daughter of Mrs. Washington." This request was then respected; but in 1865, when it was no longer necessary for their purposes, it was burned to the ground by Federal soldiers. Let us, in the spirit of charity, hope that those who applied the torch were ignorant of its history.

CHAPTER IX. GENERAL LEE BECOMES COMMANDER OF THE ARMY OF NORTHERN VIRGINIA.

IT was at the battle of "Fair Oaks," the day after the glorious battle of "Seven Pines," that General Joseph E. Johnston received so severe a wound in his shoulder, from the fragment of a shell, as to render it impossible for him to retain the command of the army. To supply the loss of one so beloved and confided in by the soldiers, all eyes turned upon General Lee. The confidence of the authorities, and of the people at large, in his abilities was unbounded; and while they deeply regretted the loss of General Johnston, and while the soldiers sorrowed much for the necessity of giving up their old commander, yet the people of Richmond, at least, breathed more freely when they knew that their safety was intrusted to their own able and God-fearing General. How he defended their city and the Confederate cause, through a long series of bloody battles, assisted by that great Christian soldier, as God-fearing as himself, the wonderful Stonewall Jackson, the brilliant young Christian cavalry officer, General J. E, B. Stuart, and an untold host of the bravest, best, most glorious warriors, both of the rank and file, which ever adorned the annals of a country's history, has been given by abler pens than ours. It is theirs to tell of the mighty military deeds which marked those seven days around Richmond; it is ours to speak of our great leader as a Christian.

It pleased the Almighty Ruler of events to give us Christians at the head of our affairs. In their prosperity they praised God for His mercies to them; in their adversity they prayed to Him, and trusted in His goodness. We have seen our President again and again bend his venerable head, and kneel humbly at the Lord's table, a recipient of the emblems of the body and blood of Christ, which are spiritually taken and received by the faithful in the Lord's Supper. Our Adjutant-General Cooper, and others of the living, walk humbly with their God, and what may not be said of Lee and Jackson, "who having fought the good fight, and finished their course," are now rejoicing in the rest prepared for the people of God. Though naturally men of very different temperaments, and members of different religious sects, their sentiments and their hearts were governed by the same living principle of duty to their Creator. "Remember the Sabbath day to keep it holy," was a command which seemed never to be forgotten by either. General Lee frequently issued Army Orders enjoining the observance of the Sabbath—commanding that nothing should be done but what was absolutely necessary for the subsistence or safety of the array, directing officers to give their men every facility for attending divine service, and urging all to make diligent use of the means of grace thus afforded them. He was always an example for good to those around him, whether at home or in the camp; always attending public worship punctually on the Sabbath, and showing reverence for the day in every particular. It was his habit, under ordinary circumstances, never to read secular books, newspapers, or even letters on that day. In his immense and important correspondence, letters would often reach him on Sunday which must be delivered at once. He would open the letters to see if it was necessary to attend to them; if not, they would be laid aside with the newspapers for inspection on Monday. The same conscientiousness was a striking characteristic of General Jackson. The observance of the Sabbath seemed never forgotten by him in the army. His habit of resting on that day while on a march, if it could be done with propriety, was universal, and, in camp, having the gospel preached regularly at his headquarters. Like General Lee, he was extremely scrupulous about reading newspapers and letters. In writing to a friend upon the subject, he says: "For fifteen years I have refused to mail letters on the Sabbath, or take them out of the office on that day, except since I came into the field; and so far from having to regret the course, it has been a source of true enjoyment, I have never sustained loss in observing what God enjoins. My rule is to let the mails remain unopened, unless they contain a dispatch." He never read a letter of friendship or compliment on Sunday, "for his Sabbaths," says his biographer, "were sacredly reserved from the smallest secular distractions," On one occasion, before he left Lexington, a letter, about which he felt deep interest, was received and placed carefully away. As he was walking to church with an intimate friend, he said to him:

"Surely, Major, you have read your letter."

"Assuredly not," said he.

"Where is it?" asked his friend.

"Here," replied Major Jackson, tapping his pocket.

"What obstinacy!" exclaimed the friend. "Do you not know that your curiosity to learn its contents will distract your attention during divine worship far more than if you had read it?"

"No," replied he. "I shall make the most faithful effort I can to govern my thoughts, and guard them from unnecessary distraction; and as I do this from a sense of duty, I expect the Divine blessing upon it." And the letter was read and enjoyed on Monday morning.

In yet another respect our two most distinguished Generals were alike in their habits. We have seen General Lee's marked abstemiousness in taking stimulating drinks. Jackson observed the same abstinence. Thus, when reconnoitring the enemy's front on one occasion in the winter of 1862, when prudence forbade the use of fire, he became so chilled that a medical attendant, in alarm for his safety, urged him to take some ardent spirit; as there was nothing else at hand, he agreed to it. As he experienced a difficulty in swallowing it, his friend asked him if it was very unpleasant. "No," said he; "no. I like it; I always did, and that is the reason I never use it." At another time, he took a long exhausting walk with a brother officer, who was also a temperate, godly man. The walk terminated at his quarters. He proposed to General Jackson, in consequence of his fatigue, to join him in a glass of brandy and water. "No," said he; "I am much obliged to you; I never use it. I am more afraid of it than I am of Federal bullets." Another point of resemblance was that habit of not only feeling, but of expressing their trust in and their dependence on an over-ruling Providence under all circumstances. It seems strange, indeed, that this habit is not more general among men professing and calling themselves Christians; but alas, alas, it is too often neglected! General Lee and General Jackson both ascribed glory to God for all blessings, and looked to Him prayerfully in all danger. They were both eminently men of prayer and faith; in every general order, in every report of victory, each gave glory to God for success, and each expressed submission to His will in the hour of defeat.

The first care of General Lee, on taking charge of the army, was to put it in a condition for an effective campaign. By the 20th of June, he brought the strength of the army of Northern Virginia to upwards of seventy thousand men.

At first, the appointment of General Lee was not popular in the army. It had great confidence in General Johnston, and was devotedly attached to him; and the partial failure of the Western Virginia campaign had placed General Lee somewhat under a cloud with the soldiers, and they were not willing to be permanently separated from their old commander. The people at large, and the soldiers, were ignorant of the great character of the man in whose hands the fate of the army was now placed; but it was not long before this feeling of doubt and uncertainty gave place to the most unbounded admiration and love for him, and by the end of June, it is thought that the troops would have mutinied, had he been taken from them. Never as the master mind of Lee more actively called forth than in this great campaign. If "success is the test of merit," as said the lamented Albert Sydney Johnston, then was our cause in the hand of the most meritorious officers and men that ever adorned the pages of history.

Never was there a more desperate conflict than that which, for seven days, crimsoned the wooded and swampy banks of the sluggish Chickahominy. To take Richmond was the burning desire of the Northern Government, and every city, town, and village within the boundaries of its mighty territory, entered warmly into the feeling. A host, innumerable for multitude, splendidly equipped, attended by all the "pomp and circumstance of grim-visaged war," were led on by the then idol of the North, the brave McClellan. The South had to oppose them with an array not to be compared in number or equipment, but composed of men of brave, determined hearts, fired by as pure and exalted patriotism as ever animated the breast of man; who fought, as they believed, for liberty or death, led on by gallant and heroic chieftains, among them that brilliant cavalry officer, J. E. B. Stuart, with a body of cavalry not a man of which, but was eager to begin the fight. He had lately returned from that daring reconnoissance which, in compliance with General Lee's orders, he had undertaken and accomplished with a picked force. They left Richmond an the 12th of June, and returned to it on the evening of the 14th. Besides gaining reliable and definite information concerning the position and strength of the Federal army, he had captured many prisoners, horses, and mules, and a number of small arms, and inflicted on the enemy the loss of millions of dollars in the destruction of stores. All this was done with the loss of but one man, the lamented Captain Latané, whose body was rescued from the enemy by his brother, who, at the risk of being captured, placed it in a mill-cart, took it to a neighboring horse and left it in the hands of ladies, who, having dressed it for the grave with the tenderness of sisters, gave it Christian burial in a family burying-ground, by the side of a brother soldier. This was done fearlessly by devoted women in the sight of the enemy, who were picketing around the plantation on which they lived, with no Confederate near them of proper age to bear arms.

The troops behaved nobly. They were in the saddle from Thursday morning until Saturday evening, never stopping for rest or food, except a brief halt on Thursday night; and this "ride around McClellan," as the soldiers called it, must ever be regarded as one of the most brilliant fests ever performed by cavalry,—the result of which determined General Lee's plan of attack, and his arrangements were made accordingly.

The glorious Seven Days came and passed away. The carnage was over. McClellan had been forced to retire to the protection of his gun-boats, thirty miles below Richmond. The city was safe, and we fondly hoped that the war would end; but the end was not yet. General Lee depicts the glory of the victory in his address to the army while in front of McClellan's position on James River. President Davis had been on the field cosstantly during six days, and had witnessed the conduct of the army. He then tendered to it the thanks of the country the following address:

TO THE ARMY OF NORTHERN VIRGINIA.

Soldiers:—I congratulate you on the series of brilliant victories which, under Divine Providence, you have lately won; and, as President of the Confederate States, do heartily tender to you the thanks of the country, whose just cause you have so skilfully and heroically served. Ten days ago, an invading army, greatly superior to you in numbers and in the material of war, closely beleaguered your Capital, and vauntingly proclaimed its speedy conquest. You marched to attack the enemy in his intrenchments; with well-directed movements and death-defying valor you charged him in his strong positions, drove him from field to field over a distance of more than thirty-five miles, and, despite his reinforcements, compelled him to seek safety under cover of his gunboats, where he now lies cowering before the army so lately derided and threatened with entire subjugation. The fortitude with which you have borne toil and privation, the gallantry with which you have entered into each successive battle, must have been witnessed to be fully appreciated; but a grateful people will not fail to recognize your deeds, and to bear you in loved remembrance. Well may it be said of you that you have "done enough for glory;" but duty to a suffering country, and to the cause of constitutional liberty, claims from you yet further efforts. Let it be your pride to relax in nothing which can promote your future efficiency,—your one great object being to drive the invader from your soil, carrying your standards beyond the outer boundary of the Confederacy, to wring from an unscrupulous foe the recognition of your birthright—community independence.

(Signed,) JEFFERSON DAVIS.

CHAPTER X. BATTLES AROUND RICHMOND.

THE beleaguered city, our beautiful Richmond, was then filled with refugees, soldiers' families, and sick and wounded soldiers, which bad almost doubled its population. We well remember how full of excitement every one seemed, and yet how calm; nor was it the calmness of despair, but of confidence in the valor of our troops, and in the blessing of God on a just cause. This feeling was not a little enhanced by the entire confidence which was everywhere felt in the guiding spirit of the army. There was an abiding feeling of security in haling him so near us.

The ever memorable 27th of June, 1862, was a day of intense excitement in the city and its surroundings. Early in the morning it was whispered that some great movement was on foot. Large numbers of troops were seen under arms awaiting orders. A. P. Hill's division occupied the hills overlooking the "Meadow Bridge," about five miles from the city, About three o'clock the order to move was given. The Fortieth Virginia led the advance. The enemy's pickets were immediately across the Chickahominy, and the men thought they were in heavy force of cavalry and infantry, and that the passage of the bridge would be hazardous in the extreme; yet their courage did not fail. The gallant Fortieth, followed by Pegram's Battery, rushed across the bridge at double-quick, and drove the enemy's pickets from their posts. The enemy was driven rapidly down the river to Mechanicsville, where the battle was raging fiercely. At nice o'clock all was quiet; the bloody struggle was over for the day.

"Our victory," says a diary kept in Richmond during the time, "was glorious, but not complete. The streets were thronged to a late hour, to catch the last accounts from couriers and spectators returning from the field. The sickening sight of the ambulances bringing in the wounded met the eye at every turn. The President and many others were on the surrounding hills during the fight, deeply interested spectators. The calmness of the people during the progress of the battle was marvellous. The balloons of the enemy hovering over the battlefield could be distinctly seen from the outskirts of the city, and the sound of musketry as distinctly heard. All were anxious, but none alarmed for the fate of the city. From the firing of the first gun till the close of the battle, every spot favorable for observation was crowded. The tops of the Exchange, the Ballard House, the Capitol, and almost every tall house, were covered with human beings; and after nightfall, the commanding hills from the President's house to the Almshouse were like a vast amphitheatre covered with men, women, and children witnessing the grand display of fireworks—beautiful, yet awful, and sending death among those whom our souls hold so dear. It was a scene of unsurpassed magnificence, the brilliant light of bombs bursting in the air and passing to the ground. The lights emitted by thousands and thousands of muskets, together with the roar of artillery and the rattling of small arms, constituted a scene terrific, grand, and imposing. What spell has bound our people? Is their trust in God, in their General, and in the valor of their troops, so great that they are unmoved by these terrible demonstrations of our powerful foe? It would seem so; for when the battle was over, the crowd dispersed and returned to their respective homes with the apparent tranquillity of persons who had been witnessing a panorama of transactions in a far-off country, in which they had no personal interest; though they knew that their countrymen slept on their arms, only awaiting the dawn to renew the deadly conflict, on the success of which depended not only the fate of our city, but of that splendid army containing the material on which our happiness depends. A crowd was out of those who were too restless and nervous to stay at home; but ah, how many full, sorrowful hearts were in their chambers besieging Heaven with prayers for our success, or else were busy in the hospitals administering to the wounded and dying."

The diary continues:

10 o'clock at night, Another day of terrible excitement in our beleaguered city. From early dawn the cannon has been roaring around us. Our success has been glorious! The citizens, gentlemen as well as ladies, have been fully occupied in the hospitals. . . . General Jackson has joined General Lee, and nearly the whole army on both sides are engaged. The carnage is frightful. The enemy had retired before our troops to their strong works near Gaines's Mill. Brigade after brigade of our brave men were hurled against them, and repulsed in disorder. General Lee was heard to say to General Jackson, "The fighting is desperate. Can our men stand it?" Jackson replied: "General, I know our boys; they wiil never give back." In a short time a large part of our force was brought up in one grand attack, and then the enemy was entirely routed. . . . Visions of the battle-field have haunted me all day. Our loved ones, whether friends or strangers,—all Southern soldiers are dear to us,—lying dead or dying; the wounded in the hot sun; the dead hastily buried, McClellan is said to be retreating. "Praise the Lord, O my soul!"

June 30th. McClellan certainly retreating. We begin to breathe more freely; but he fights as he goes. Oh, that he may be surrounded before he gets to the gun-boats! Rumors are flying about that he is surrounded; but we do not believe it,—only hope that it may be so, before he reaches the river. The city is sad because of the dead and wounded; but our hearts are filled with gratitude to God for His mercies. The end is not yet; oh, that it were! Richmond is disenthralled—the only Federals here are in the Libby and other prisons.

This journal gives the true idea of the confidence felt by the people in their Generals and army, and above in the blessing of God on a cause which we believed to be righteous, and for which we were not afraid to ask His help. We knew that our commanding General looked to God for His guidance, and we believed that it would be granted him.

The Rev. Dr. Dabney, in his Life of Jackson, says: "The demeanor of the citizens during the evening (June 26th), gave us an example of their courage, and their faith in their leaders and their cause.["]

For many weeks the Christians of the city had given themselves to prayer; and they drew from Heaven a sublime composure. The spectator passing through the streets saw the people calmly engaged in their usual avocations, or else wending their way to the churches, while the thunders of the cannon shook the city. As the calm summer evening descended, the family groups were seen sitting upon the door-steps, where mothers told the children at their knees how Lee and his heroes were now driving away the invaders. The young people promenaded the heights north of the town, and watched the distant shells bursting against the sky. At one church a solemn cavalcade stood waiting; and if the observer had entered, saying to himself, "This funeral reminds me that Death claims all seasons for his own, and refuses to postpone his dread rites for any inferior honors," he would have found a, bridal at the altar! The heart of old Rome was not more assured or steadfast, when she sold for full price in her Forum the field on which the Carthaginian was encamped.

Such were the correct statements of the situation of Richmond during these days of bloodshed. Prayer was the vital breath of every Christian in the city, and God gave them strength to bear their own sorrows, and to minister to the necessities of others.

About the 8th of July the troops were allowed to go into camp to rest, after their wonderfully successful campaign. Thus had General Lee, in the beginning of his career, been instrumental in saving the Capital of the Confederacy. The people lauded and almost worshipped him as their deliverer. He received the homage with the quiet and calm dignity which always characterized him. He never showed great elation, but the gravity which became the great Christian leader, who felt the responsibility of his situation. He knew that be had a great work to do, and that what he had passed through was but the successful prelude to the eventful scenes which were before him. His country's very existence was at stake, and all eyes were turned on him with full confidence, as one competent to save it from threatened ruin. And nobly did he execute all that was in the power of man to that end; and that he failed at last must be attributed to circumstances which could not be averted by human skill! That he succeeded so long and so well is due to what appears to have been more than human genius, commanding armies which have been rarely equalled, never surpassed.

General Lee remained near Richmond, observing the motions of General McClellan, when intelligence reached him of the movements on the upper waters of the Rappahannock. General Pope, with a large army, evidently designed a disastrous attack upon Gordonsville, at the junction of the two principal railroads. They were plundering, burning, and producing general disaster. General Jackson was immediately sent to stop their progress, with his corps consisting of Jackson's and Ewell's divisions. This has been called a "war of wits" between General Lee and the authorities at Washington. Lee watched Pope and McClellan to discover the real design of the enemy. General McClellan still remaining inactive, on the 27th of July A. P. Hill's division was sent to reinforce Jackson, who, on the 2d of August, attacked the enemy at Orange Court-House.

On the 5th, McClellan made a demonstration towards Malvern Hill, to prevent Lee seeding reinforcements to the Rappahannock. General Lee promptly went to meet him, and a slight engagement occurred at Curie's Neck; but the next morning the Federal army had retired, and the whole movement proved to be a, feint. The eagle eye of Lee now seeing that the real design of the enemy was upon the Rappahannock, he soon directed his attention to that quarter. General Jackson had already struck an important blow in attacking Pope at Cedar Run. The struggle was obstinate, but the Confederates were left in possession of the field. This success, and their slow but sure advance, alarmed the authorities at Washington. The Confederates were approaching too near their city, and McClellan was hastily called from the James to the assistance of Pope. General Lee immediately sent large reinforcements to the Rappahannock, and soon after followed them. Then followed the wonderful flank movement which brought the armies in contact, and which resumed in the second victory on the plains of Maryland. Thus ended the great campaign of the summer of 1862, the whole success of which reflects never-dying lustre on the great mind which planned it, As usual, he gives glory to God for his successes. His announcement by telegraph runs thus:

TO PRESIDENT DAVIS,

The army achieved, to-day, on the plains of Manassas, a signal victory over the combined forces of Pope and McClellan. On the 28th, 29th, and 30th, each wing, under Generals Longstreet and Jackson, repulsed with valor attacks made by them separately. We mourn the loss of our gallant dead in every conflict, yet our gratitude to Almighty God for his mercies rises higher each day. To Him, and to the valor of our troops, a nation's gratitude is due.

R. E. LEE.

How well it is remembered with what heartfelt gratitude and joy these telegrams, signed R. E, Lee, filled us, when they brought good tidings, and with what sorrow, when the news was adverse! Other telegrams might give false impressions—sometimes they were too elating, sometimes too desponding—but General Lee knew the truth, and dispassionately, and in the fear of God, gave it to the country. The President appointed Thursday, the 18th of September, as a day of thanksgiving for our victories. He issued a beautiful "proclamation" on the subject. Every church of every denomination of Christians, that could be opened, was filled that day with grateful worshippers. Our leaders, and many of our people, were mindful of our dependence upon Providence, and remembered that "when Moses held up his hand, then Israel prevailed, and when he let down his hand, then Amalek prevailed." And was it that our "hands were let down," that our cause was finally lost? It is sad to think that it may have been so. Jackson and Stuart, and a host of Christian soldiers, were taken from the evil to come; even in the flush of victory; but General Lee was spared to show the world how a Christian can bear defeat—how, when he has done his best, and God has allowed the worst to come—how, when the hopeless struggle was over, he could, with God's help, gird on a new courage, not to contend, but to endure. There is a sad pleasure in thinking of our Christian heroes, both of the rank and file, who now sleep the sleep of death, to be aroused by no reveille, until the resurrection morn, when the trump of the archangel shall sound, and the "dead in Christ shall rise first." The bright and chivalrous Stuart died in the triumph of the faith which he had professed long before; amid all the sufferings of his dying body, he joined the man of God, who ministered to him and prayed for him, with his feeble voice in singing a favorite hymn. Soon after his wonderful raid around McClellan's army, a youthful soldier, who had been one of his guides through the entangled thickets of the Chickahominy, and who was interesting the passengers of a railroad car with an animated account of his hair-breadth escapes by flood and field, concluded by saying, "In all the tight places that the General got into, I never heard him swear an oath, and I never saw him drink a drop." Mrs. Stuart, the General's wife, was one of the amused auditors of the enthusiastic narrator. As soon as she could do so without being observed, she leaned forward, introduced herself to the youth, and asked him if he knew why General Stuart never swears nor drinks? The youth answered in the negative. She replied, "It is because he is a Christian, and loves God; and nothing would induce him to do what he thinks wrong; and I want you, and all of his soldiers, to follow his example."

CHAPTER XI. LEE CROSSES THE BORDER.

IMMEDIATELY after the second battle of Manassas, General Lee led his troops into Maryland. The country looked on with the perfect confidence which it always felt in its great leader. By the 7th of September, the whole army was on the Maryland side of the Potomac. Western Maryland was loyal to the Union; hence it was necessary that the soldiers should be under strict orders to respect private property, and severe punishment was threatened to those who attempted to pillage or destroy. They paid for whatever was wanted, with Confederate money. They had no other, and the venders seemed willing to receive it. Compensation was made for the fence-rails which the troops were sometimes tempted to burn; and they were required to treat persons of Union principles with consideration. The Northern soldiers were amazed; they had, true to the maxim that "all thing are fair in war," just devastated the bright fields of Virginia, burned houses and barns, destroyed furniture aid things most precious to the people, with impunity. Now, they saw soldiers obeying their General, who governed by no worldly law, but by the rule of Christians—"Do unto others as you would they should do unto you." "It must have been a. proud moment for General Lee," says McCabe, in his "Life of General Lee," "when he saw this; for he mist have known that his troops were influenced as much by their love for him, as by their sense of right and justice." He published an address to the people of Maryland, inviting them to join him; but few came to his standard. The people of Eastern and Southern Maryland were friendly to the South, but the Federal army lay between them and the Confederates. Baltimore, too, was filled with Southern sympathizers, but he could not get to them, nor they to him, so that the troops were at first bitterly disappointed. Then came the capture of Harper's Ferry by General Jackson; the battles of South Mountain and Sharpsburg, fought with such valor on both sides, and with such losses to both. General Lee, then finding that nothing more could be effected by remaining, withdrew across the Potomac at once. McCabe quotes the New York Tribune, to show the feeling of disappointment evinced by the North, when the masterly withdrawal of the Southern commander became known. "He leaves us," it said, "the débris of his late camps, two disabled pieces of cannon, a few hundred of his stragglers, perhaps two thousand of his wounded, and as many more of his unburied dead. Not a sound field-piece, caisson, ambulance, or wagon; not a box of stores, or pound of ammunition. He takes with him the supplies gathered in .Maryland, and the rich spoils of Harper's Ferry."

The troops were withdrawn to the vicinity of Winchester for rest, of which they were much in need. There they enjoyed the bracing mountain air, with all the freedom, fun, and frolic incident to camp-life. General Lee's care now was to have them supplied with shoes and other quartermaster's stores necessary for their comfort. The stragglers came back, and in the course of two weeks the army was increased by the arrival of about thirty thousand fresh troops.

In October, we find General Lee moving his troops to prevent another. "On to Richmond," and on the 13th of December a mighty pitched battle was fought at Fredericksburg, The Federal force was in overwhelming numbers under General Burnside, who superseded the brave, but unfortunate McClellan. This battle was a most decided Confederate success, and the great Federal army was kept at bay on the north side of the Rappahannock during the winter of

1862–63.

Lee now reigned supreme in the confidence and hearts of both soldiers and people from the Potomac to the Gulf of Mexico, and yet he seemed "clothed with humility." How mightily did the grace of God reign in his heart, when, as it were, from the very pinnacle of fame, he bowed his head humbly before Him, giving Him the glory, and praising Him for having given victory to his country, and praying for His guidance that he might guide others. "In the hour of victory," says one of his staff officers, "he was grand, imposing, awe-inspiring, yet self-forgetful and humble." We are at a loss whether to admire more his humility in victory or his dignity in defeat. His great nature, purified by grace, made him the "praise of the whole earth;" yet, feeling his own sinfulness, in his deep humility, he expressed himself, a short time before his death, as feeling utterly unworthy to enter into the "rest prepared for the people of God."

His headquarters during this victorious winter differed in no particular from the quarters of the private soldiers. It was a tent pitched in the woods near Hamilton's Crossings, surrounded by the tents of the staff officers. There was no appearance of a body-guard, with the exception of an orderly who always waited to summon couriers to carry dispatches. No one would have known that this unpretending group of tents was the army headquarters. His tent contained nothing but what was indispensable; no article of luxury was there. The General covered himself with the ordinary army blanket; and many men and officers, whose warm-hearted friends would supply luxuries to them, fared better than he. The heart of the South was open to him; and though its citizens were very poor, yet they were self-denying, and boxes filled with luxuries of all sorts were sent to him; but he generally sent them to the hospitals around, to contribute to the comfort of the sick and wounded. Thus did he set an example to his officers, of enduring hardship for the sake of the cause, and of self-denial for the good of others; he was too good a Christian in war as in peace to be self-indulgent, though he was ever cheerful and social.

We have seen him after the war was over, at watering-places, in attendance upon his sick wife, the observed of all observers, followed, caressed, courted; dressed in his plain, but neatly-fitting suit of gray cloth, and spotless linen. He was perhaps the most quiet and unostentatious man at the place. He entered freely into society, and seemed to enjoy it, particularly that of the ladies; but he never forgot or neglected those who came for the healing of the waters; to them he was always benevolently, soothingly attentive, having a kind word for all. From a religious service he was never absent, and was ever a most devout and zealous worshipper.

During the war, while the army was near Richmond, where his family lived, he would frequently ride into the city at night; and no one would know that he was nearer than the camp, until sunrise would bring the early worshippers together, to ask God's blessing on their country, then would the stately form and venerable head (for anxiety and exposure had now turned his dark locks gray) of General Lee be invariably found among them. He was never missing from the morning prayer-meeting, if in the city; and when his official business for which he came would be over, or if he had come to spend the Sabbath with his family and to attend the services of the sanctuary, and the day of rest had passed away, he would depart as quietly and unostentatiously as lie came. Not unfrequently, when the inquiry was made, "Is General Lee still in the city?" the answer would be, "No; he must have gone, as he was not at prayer-meeting this morning."

This reminds me of an anecdote of a lady, who, passing a group of rough-looking soldiers waiting at the Transportation Office, said to them,

"Gentlemen, whom do you suppose I have seen this morning?"

In answer to their inquiring looks, she replied, "General Lee."

"General Lee!" they exclaimed. "We did not know he was in town. God bless him!"

"Where do you suppose I saw him so early?"

"Where, Madam, where?"

"At prayer-meeting; down upon his knees praying for you and for the country."

In an instant they seemed subdued; tears started to the eyes of these hardy, sunburnt veterans. Some were utterly silent, while others exclaimed, "God bless him!" "God bless his old soul!" The lady walked on, but was followed by several to know where he was to be seen. One 1 in.d never seen him at all, and wanted to see him monstrous bad." Others had seen him often, but wanted to see him again, "just to look at him." They were told to go to Franklin. Street; but they could not leave the Transportation Office, as they were waiting their "turn" for transportation tickets; and they probably did not get the much-desired sight of their venerated General.

That General Lee was a man of much prayer and great faith, none could doubt who knew his exemplary life; but probably few of his most intimate friends fully understood the depth of his feelings on this subject. He was a man of great reserve, and only his actions, and an occasional outburst of feeling, showed the whole-souled follower of the Saviour. There can be no doubt but that faith in God's providence, and reliance on the Almighty arm, were the foundations of all his actions, and the secret springs of his supreme composure under all trials. Good men have said that when they visited him, and conversed with him on the subject of religion, they would leave him with their hearts burning within them.

When the Rev. J. Wm. Jones and another chaplain went, in 1863, to consult him in reference to the better observance of the Sabbath in the army, he says that the "General's countenance glowed with pleasure, and his eye brightened; and, as in his simple, feeling words he expressed his delight, we forgot the great warrior, and only remembered that we were communing with an humble, earnest Christian."

When he was informed that the chaplains prayed for him, tears started to his eyes, as he replied, "I sincerely thank you for that; and can only say that I am a poor sinner, trusting in Christ alone, and need all the prayers you can offer for me."

The day after this interview, he issued an earnest general order, enjoining on the officers and men the observance of the Sabbath; urging them to attend public worship in their camps, and forbidding the performance of official duties, unless essential to the subsistence or safety of the army. He always attended public worship, if it were in his power to do so; and often the earnestness of the preacher would make his eye kindle and his face glow." He frequently attended the meetings of the chaplains, took a warm interest in their proceeding's, and uniformly exhibited an ardent desire for the promotion of religion in the army.

When General Meade came over to Mine Run, and the Southern army marched out to meet him, Lee was riding along the line of battle in the woods, when he came upon a party of soldiers holding a prayer-meeting on the eve of battle. Such. a spectacle was not unusual in the army then, and afterwards; some of these rough fighters were men of profound piety. On this occasion, the scene before him seems to have excited deep emotion in General Lee. He stopped, dismounted; the staff officers attending him did the same. He uncovered his head, and stood in an attitude of profound attention and respect, while the earnest prayer proceeded in the midst of the thunder of artillery and explosion of the enemy's shell.

The early spring of 1863 found General Lee still on the south of Fredericksburg. While he watched the Federal army with an eagle eye, he prepared his own to meet it. Can we doubt that this man of God prayed much to the Ruler of all events to direct and guide his steps? The country looked on with anxiety to the opening of the spring campaign.

General Hooker, who had superseded Burnside, now led the Federal hosts. He had proved himself a most accomplished corps commander; and now the United States looked to him with confidence to overcome the comparatively small army which opposed him, and to nuke his "On to Richmond" quick work.

During the month of April he was preparing for the great campaign. His cavalry made many efforts to unmask Lee's position and learn his strength; but Gen. Stuart was equally vigilant in guarding the fords of the Rappahannock, and preventing its crossing.

On the 30th of April, however, the main force of the Federals, under personal command of Hooker, crossed the river, and now commenced concentrating about Chancellorsville. Lee's force seemed scattered; and, it is said, there was some excuse for Hooker's expressions of joy when he saw his own immense force collecting. He is said to have exclaimed, "The rebel army is the legitimate property of the Army of the Potomac. They may as well pack up their haversacks and make for Richmond, and I shall be after them." But the Southern army was steadily moving forward, with the hope of victory stamped on every brow.

Then followed the battle of Chancellorsville, which was fought and won by the South. But while the air was rent with the shouts of victory, one message of sorrow came over the wires which made the Confederacy pause in its delirium of joy—General Jackson was wounded! Every countenance grew pale with apprehension; yet no one believed he would die. The idea could not for a moment be borne—no one expressed it. All hearts turned to God for help; prayers for his recovery were on every lip. The language of every heart was, "Surely God will not take him away from us in our great necessity." But the fiat had gone forth; and God removed him from the evil to come.

The day of victory closed, and at ten o'clock at night he was shot in the arm by a brigade of his own men. He was returning to his lines with his escort, without giving warning, and the fatal shot was fired by men who had been ordered to look out for Federal cavalry. The mistake was made in the mistiness of moonlight; and the whole escort, with the exception of two men, were killed, wounded, or dismounted. When he had been carried to the rear, his situation was immediately communicated to Gen. Lee, who exclaimed, with deep feeling, "Thank God it is no worse! God be praised he is still alive! Any victory is a dear one, which deprives us of the services of General Jackson, even for a time."

Later in the day, when he heard of the amputation of his left arm, he wrote to him the following note, full of sympathy, which proved most comforting to the wounded hero:

GENERAL:—I have just received your note informing me that you were wounded. I cannot express my regret at the occurrence. Could I have directed events, I should have chosen, for the good of the country, to have been disabled in your stud. I congratulate you upon the victory, which is due to your skill and energy.

R. E. LEE, General.

CHAPTER XII. CHANCELLORSVILLE, AND DEATH OF GENERAL JACKSON.

THE fighting was continued for three days longer, and on the 5th of May General Lee reported to President Davis: "We have reoccupied Fredericksburg, and no enemy remains south of the Rappahannock, or in its vicinity."

The campaign was over, but the victory was too dearly won. General Jackson died of pneumonia, the result of his wounds, on Sunday, the 10th of May.

On the 7th, General Lee had issued an address to the army, appointing Sunday, the 10th, as a day for the troops to unite in returning thanks to God for the victory. His words were, "While this glorious victory entitles you to the praise and gratitude of the nation, we are especially called upon to return our grateful thanks to the only Giver of victory for the signal deliverance He has wrought. It is therefore earnestly recommended that the troops unite on Sunday next in ascribing unto the Lord of Hosts the glory due unto His name." Then he communicates to the army the following letter from President Davis, as an expression of his appreciation of the victory:

I have received your dispatch, and reverently unite with you in giving praise to God for the success with which He has crowned our arms. In the name of the people, I offer my cordial thanks to the troops under your command for their addition to the unprecedented series of great victories which our army has achieved. The universal rejoicing caused by this happy result will be mingled with a general regret for the good and the brave who are numbered among the killed and wounded.

While the army was engaged in returning thanks for the victory, and doubtlessly praying, earnestly praying, for the restoration of "Lee's great lieutenant," of whom he was wont to speak as his "right arm," the redeemed spirit of General Jackson winged its way to the bosom of the God who gave it, to the Saviour who redeemed it, and to the Holy Spirit who sanctified it. He "walked with God, and was not; for God took him." The nation wept and mourned for him, rind could not be comforted.

The personal relations between Lee and Jackson had been of the most friendly character; their admiration for each other was without the blemish of selfishness; each accorded to the other the praise due him. The dazzling fame of Jackson did not disturb the great soul of Lee. He rejoiced in it as a blessing to his country.

"Say to General Jackson," he said to a young staff officer who came with a message, "that he knows just as well what to do with the enemy as I do."

The tone of the messages sent by him, when Jackson lay wounded, were both affectionate and familiar, showing the feeling that existed between them. "Give him my affectionate regards, and tell him to make haste and get well, and come back to me as soon as he can. He has lost his left arm, but I have lost my right."

When it became reported that the wound might prove fatal, Lee was greatly shocked, and exclaimed with deep feeling, "Surely General Jackson must recover! God will not take him from us, now that we need him so much. Surely he will be spared to us in answer to the many prayers which are offered for him."

Then pausing in deep emotion, he added, after a silence of some moments, to the young officer who made the sad communication to him:

When you return, I trust you will find him better. When a suitable season offers, give him my love, and tell him I wrestled in prayer for him last night as I never prayed, I believe, for myself.

In a day or two, it became necessary for him to issue a general order, which must have caused him one of the bitterest pangs of which his heart was capable. It was as follows:

With deep grief, the Commanding General announces to the army the death of Lieutenant-General T. J. Jackson, who expired on the 10th instant, at a quarter past three P.M. The daring skill and energy of this great and good soldier, by the decree of an all-wise Providence, are now lost to us. But while we mourn his death, we feel that his spirit lives, and will inspire the army with his indomitable courage and unshaken confidence in God as our hope and strength. Let his name be a watchword to his corps, who have followed him to victory in so many fields. Let his officers and soldiers emulate his invincible determination to do everything in defence of our beloved country.

R. E. LEE.

That the sentiments of Lee for Jackson were fully reciprocated by Jackson, there can be no doubt. He regarded him rot only as a great soldier, but as a good Christian; and his love and admiration for him were known by his friends to be almost unbounded. He was always the warm defender against those who found fault with Lee; for even he could not in all respects escape calumny.

He was once spoken of, before General Jackson, as being "slow." In a moment he became indignant, and exclaimed, "General Lee is not 'slow.' No one knows the weight upon his heart—his great responsibilities. He is commander-in-chief; and he knows that if an army is lost, it cannot be replaced. No! there may be some persons whose good opinion of me may make them attach some weight to my views; and if you ever hear that said of General Lee, I beg you will contradict it in my name. I have known General Lee for five-and-twenty years. He is cautious. He ought to be. But he is not 'slow.' Lee is a phenomenon. He is the only man whom I would follow blindfold."

Soon after the battle of Chancellorsville, General Lee determined again to cross the Potomac; and by the 1st of June he was ready for the advance. His masterly strategy in less than two weeks drew the Federal army from the Rappahannock to the upper Potomac; and he was now preparing to cross into Maryland, and thence to Pennsylvania. This movement led to the disastrous, but bravely fought battle of Gettysburg. The account of the battle does not belong to this little volume; but we love to dwell on the humanity and kindness exercised by General Lee and his officers during the march through the enemy's country. Strict orders were issued to the men to respect private property; and the fidelity with which the guards discharged their duty is shown by a biographer of General Lee in a single instance. "A trooper, with a half-starved horse, keeping watch over a wheat-field, prevented his own horse from cropping the grain."

"No burning homestead," said the Hon. Reverdy Johnson, –illumined his march; no shivering and helpless children were turned out of their homes to witness their destruction by the torch. With him all the rules of civilized war, having the higher sanction of God, were strictly observed."

A Northern correspondent of the day spoke of it in praise. "It must be confessed, that though there were over sixty acres of wheat, and eighty of oats and corn in the same field, it was most carefully protected; and the horses were picketed so that it could not be injured. No fences were wantonly destroyed; poultry was not disturbed; nor did the soldiers our blooded cattle so much as to test the quality of a steak or roast."

Many of the troops were very restive under these orders.

"My fingers itched," said a plain soldier, "just to burn down two houses, one to pay for my own, and the other for my brother's home that the Yankees burnt on Mississippi River, but Mass Bob said I must n't, and so I did n't."

A Southern newspaper at the time seemed to partake of the same feeling, and remarked sarcastically, "General Lee becomes irate at the robbing of a cherry-tree, and if he sees that the top rail of a fence has been thrown down, he will dismount and replace it with his own hands."

He issued an order while at Chambersburg, Pennsylvania, in which he expresses to the troops the "marked satisfaction with which he has observed their conduct during their march," and warns them that the "duties required by civilization and Christianity are as obligatory in the enemy's country as our own." . . . "It must be remembered," he continued, "that we make war only on armed men, and that we cannot take vengeance for the wrongs our people have suffered without lowering ourselves in the eyes of all whose abhorrence has been excited by the atrocities of our enemy, and offending against Him to whom vengeance belongeth, without whose favor and support our efforts must all prove vain. The Commanding General, therefore, earnestly exhorts the troops to abstain, with most scrupulous care, from unnecessary or wanton injury to private property; and he enjoins upon all officers to arrest and bring to summary punishment all who shall in any way offend against the orders on the subject."

None but a Christian could have issued such an order under such circumstances. He had been robbed of his property; had seen his invalid wife and young daughters refugees from the beautiful home of their inheritance; had seen the down-trodden fields and burning dwellings of his own State; had heard the wail of woe from the captive cities of the far South; and while his heart burned within him at the wrongs of his people, by the grace of God, he was enabled to rise nobly above human nature and by his example to exalt the army above the feelings which would have prompted them to lay waste and to destroy, and to return in full measure, the ills which had been inflicted on them. None but one born of the Spirit, Heaven-taught and Heaven-directed, could have exercised such Christian forbearance.

The old question, Is it right in the sight of God? naturally arose to his mind, and decided his course here, as it had done through his whole life; and he went on through the rich valleys of Pennsylvania, not to victory over the troops of the enemy,—that was denied him there,—but exercising that victory over evil, that power of ruling his own spirit and the spirits of other men, which proved him to be far "greater than he that taketh a city."

CHAPTER XIII. GENERAL LEE AFTER THE DEFEAT AT GETTYSBURG.

THE advance to Gettysburg and the desperate fight are left to the historian. The Southern soldiers had fought well, and when repulsed, their leader mounted his war-horse Traveller and rode forward to meet and encourage his retreating troops. The air was filled with bursting shells, and the men were coming back without order. General Lee met them, and with his staff officers busied himself in rallying them, uttering, as he did so, words of hope and encouragement.

Colonel Freemantle,—an officer of the English army, who was a spectator of the fight, and who seems to have noticed General Lee with an admiring eye,—describes his conduct at this moment as being "perfectly sublime. Lee's countenance," he adds, "did not give signs of the slightest disappointment, care, or annoyance, but preserved the utmost placidity and cheerfulness. He rode slowly to and fro, saving in his grave, kindly voice to the men, 'All this will come right in the end; we'll talk it over hereafter; but in the meantime all good men must rally. We want all true and good men now.' They did rally, and even some of the wounded returned with cheers for their beloved commander."

Colonel Freemantle adds in his diary, that General Lee was fully alive, to the extent of the disaster, and said to him, "This has been a sad day to us, Colonel; but we can't expect always to have victory." And yet when General Wilcox came to report the failure, scarcely able to articulate with emotion, he said, cheerfully, "Never mind, General; all this has been my fault. It is I that have lost this fight, and you must help me out of it the best way you can."

The English officer spoken of above seems lost in admiration of the affection and confidence shown him by the men in their hour of defeat. He quotes in his diary their homely phraseology in speaking of him: "We've not lost confidence in the old man. This day's work won't do him any harm. Uncle Robert will get us to Washington yet; you bet he will," etc. The men loved him with devotion, because he loved them, sympathized in their sorrows, and always spoke kindly to them. Other great warriors have treated their soldiers as machines with which to execute their plans; but General Lee treated them as men and brothers. To the wounded he gave sympathy, to all kind words.

Immediately after this fight he returned to Virginia, and rested his army upon the banks of the Opequan.

At this time, Colonel Freemantle describes General Lee as "almost the handsomest man, of his age, I ever saw. He is tall, broad-shouldered, very well made, well set up, a thorough soldier in his appearance; and his manners are most courteous and full of dignity. He is a perfect gentleman in every respect. I imagine no man has so few enemies, or is so universally esteemed. Throughout he South, all agree in pronouncing him as near perfection as a man can be. He has none of the small vices, such as smoking and chewing; and his bitterest enemy has never accused him of any of the greater ones. He generally wore a long gray jacket, a high felt hat, and blue trousers tucked into his Wellington boots. I never saw him carry arms; and the only marks of his military rank are the three stars on his collar. He rides a handsome horse, which is extremely well governed. He himself is very neat in his dress and person; and in the most arduous marches he always looks smart and clean. . . . It is understood that General Lee is a religious man, though not so demonstrative in that respect as Jackson; and, unlike his brother-in-arms, he is a member of the Church of England. His only faults, as far as I can learn, arise from his excessive amiability."

Such is the very correct sketch of the English officer; but the Englishman did not realize that his fault of "excessive amiability," was the gift of God through His Spirit, engrafted on a gentle but high-toned nature.

The failure at Gettysburg was a sore disappointment to the South, but no one blamed General Lee. It was thought right that he should carry the war into the enemy's country; and his want of success was mourned over, and the country sympathized with but never censured him. Confidence in and love for him increased, and the people meekly bowed in submission to His will who had not seen fit to crown the efforts of our brave troops with victory.

The 21st of August was appointed by the President as a day of fasting, humiliation, and prayer. It was faithfully observed by the Confederacy.

From his return to Virginia General Lee had most successfully kept the Federal army at bay, and in December, 1863, we find him in winter-quarters at Orange Court-House.

Very pleasing accounts have been given of these quarters. The tent of the General in the middle, with those of the staff around it. The couriers amused themselves by cutting out and fashioning walks from one to the other. His staff was composed of gentlemen of fine soldierly qualities and courteous manners, making a delightful society in the woods. They lived on most harmonious terms with their General. They loved and revered him the more for being thrown with him intimately and without ceremony. He was free from the little weaknesses which disenchant the character of great men as we approach and enter into the recesses of every-day life.

General John B. Gordon, in his address made at Atlanta, Georgia, immediately after General Lee's death, says of him, "I declare it here to-day, that, of any mortal man whom it has been my privilege to approach, he was the greatest; and I assert here, that, grand as might be your conceptions of the man before, he arose in incomparable majesty on more familiar acquaintance. This can be affirmed of few men who have ever lived or died, and of no other man whom it has ever been my fortune to approach."

During this winter a revival of religion took place in his army, the extent of which was almost unprecedented. The gray-bearded veteran and the boyish soldier knelt together under the roof constructed by the men for houses of worship composed of evergreens. General Lee entered heartily into their feelings, went among them, joined them in prayer, conversed with and encouraged their chaplains, asked earnestly for their prayers, and in every way showed the deepest interest in their work. He was never demonstrative in his nature, and his religion was of that quiet kind, which was more conspicuous in action than word; but he felt too deeply his dependence on God's guidance, not to solicit the prayers of the humblest chaplain of the army.

Meat was becoming more and more scarce during this winter, and the soldiers' rations were greatly diminished. The General chose to fare no better than his men, and had meat on his table but twice a week. "His ordinary dinner," says a newspaper of the day, "consisted of cabbage boiled in salt and water, and a pone of corn bread."

The same paper tells an anecdote of the General's having invited a number of gentlemen to dine with him; in a fit of extravagance he ordered a sumptuous repast of middling and cabbage. The dinner was served; and behold, a great pile of cabbage, and a bit of middling about four inches long and two inches wide! The guests, with commendable politeness, unanimously declined, middling, and it remained in the dish untouched. The next day, the

General, remembering the delicate tit-bit, ordered his servant to bring that middling. The servant hesitated in some confusion, but at last owned that the middling was borrowed, and he had returned it to its owner. The exact truth of the anecdote cannot be positively asserted; but that General Lee considered that the use of meat more than twice a week was wrong while the country was so impoverished, cannot be doubted; and that he followed the dictates of conscience, and denied himself the use of it except when the soldiers could have it, is equally certain.

CHAPTER XIV. GENERAL LEE'S DISINTERESTEDNESS AND SELF-DENIAL.

IT was in November, 1863, that the City Council of Richmond determined to present General Lee with a handsome residence in that city. A large sum for the purpose was raised; but, unfortunately, the plan got into the newspapers, and was seen by General Lee, who immediately addressed the following note to the

PRESIDENT OF THE CITY COUNCIL, Richmond, Va.

Sir:—My attention has been directed to a resolution reported in the newspapers as having been introduced into the body over which you preside, having for its object the purchase, by the city of Richmond, of a house for the use of my family. I assure you, sir, that no want of appreciation of the honor conferred upon me by this resolution, or insensibility to the kind feelings which prompted it, induces me to ask, as I most respectfully do, that no farther proceedings be taken with reference to the subject. The horse is not necessary to the use of my family, and my own duties will prevent my residence in Richmond. I should, therefore, be compelled to decline the generous offer, and trust that whatever means the City Council may have to spare for this purpose may be devoted to the relief of the families of our soldiers in the field, who are more in want of assistance and more deserving of it than myself.

I have the honor to be, most respectfully,

Your obedient servant,

ROBERT E. LEE.

Nothing could have been more disinterested than this refusal of a home for his family, who were now living in a rented house, dependent on his pay as General in the Confederate service; but he was firm in his refusal, preferring that the families of the soldiers should be cared for. Poor fellows! they needed all the assistance that could be given them, and their General was more than willing to deny himself for their good.

It was at this time of privation that General Lee issued the following order to his suffering troops:

HEADQUARTERS ARMY OF NORTHERN VIRGNIA,

January 22, 1864.

GENERAL ORDER, NO. 7.

The Commanding General considers it due to the army to state that the temporary reduction of rations has been caused by circumstances beyond the control of those charged with its support. Its welfare and comfort are the objects of his constant and earnest solicitude, and no effort has been spared to provide for its wants. It is hoped that the exertions now being made will render the necessity of short duration; but the history of the army has shown that the country can require no sacrifice too great for its patriotic devotion.

Soldiers! You tread with no unequal steps the road by which your fathers marched through suffering, privation, and blood to independence! Continue to emulate in the future, as you have in the past, their valor in arms, their patient endurance of hardships, their high resolve to be free, which no trial could shake, no bribe seduce, no danger appall; and be assured that the just

God who crowned their efforts with success, will, in His own good time, send down His blessings upon yours.

R. E. LEE, General.

It is related of him by a member of his staff, showing his habits of abstemiousness and self-denial, that frequently, when a particularly nice piece of beef or mutton, which he always enjoyed, was on the table, and he was asked to partake further, he would invariably decline, saying, "I should really enjoy another piece, but I have had my allowance." His forgetfulness of self had always been a conspicuous trait in his character, which readily accounts for the love borne him by all of every rank with whom he associated.

From letters addressed by a lady to Mrs. Lee after her husband's death, we make the following extracts:

"During the war, when General Lee's thoughtful consideration for the comfort of others, even at the cost of his own,—when his habitual self-denial was the theme of every tongue,—with a very natural pride, I often told of the first time I had ever seen your husband. It was shortly before the war with Mexico, when he was Captain Lee, and attending a meeting of engineers at Newport. Doctor —— and myself were spending the summer there. My husband met with Captain Lee at an evening party, and came home charmed with having made his acquaintance. We left Newport the day after. There had been a great disaster recently to one of the steamboats on the Sound; besides, the navigation of it was considered dangerous. I had heard quite enough to make a sick woman anxious and nervous, and when the boat from Boston arrived, my consternation was complete. Instead of one of the large steamers commonly used on the Sound, it proved to be the Curtis Peck, a small river-boat which I had seen in Virginia on the James River. To add to my dismay, it was late in the evening, and a fog rapidly advancing, an element of danger in rounding Point Judith. The boat was filled to its utmost capacity. Besides the passengers from Boston and Newport, a large number of soldiers were on board, from Fort Adams, to be sent to some other station. The ladies' apartment was on deck; and as I stood at the door, looking at the numbers within and without, I felt utterly disconsolate. My husband soon approached with Captain Lee, to whom I was introduced. Need I tell you that he had then reached that type of manly beauty which captivated every eye, and that the highest charm of his splendid face was something superior to the mere perfection of his noble features? He soon realized how intensely anxious I was; indeed, the solicitude was felt by all on board. Never can I forget the tender way in which he tried to allay my fears. To divert my mind, he talked of many things; and to this day I can recall the tones of his voice, and the tenderness not to be described, as he spoke of his wife and little children at Arlington. We were soon nearly out to sea; it had been rough in the bay, and Dr. —— was suffering so much from sea-sickness that he left the cabin, which was literally packed with human beings, and came upon deck for fresh air. The soldiers had procured a very comfortable sleeping-place on deck for their Captain. Before I had been introduced, he entreated my husband to take possession of it. As he persisted most positively in refusing to accept the kind offer, the Captain turned to me and begged me to use my influence, saying everything he could to convince us that it would be no sacrifice to himself, and ended by declaring that, if no one else would occupy the place, he should not—a determination in which he was inflexible, as we found the next morning that he had induced a young officer, also suffering from sea-sickness, to accept his kindness, and he had himself walked the deck all night. The manner in which the offer was made has never been effaced from our minds; and we have often rejoiced that our first insight into his character presented to us the germ of that unselfishness which afterwards expanded into such noble proportions, as to constitute one of his claims to the admiration of mankind."

Another letter from this lady speaks of him as she knew him a few months before his death. They were then both visitors at the Hot Springs.

"It was obvious," she writes, "that the General felt he had a mission to perform, which he did with all his might. There were many instances made known to my husband, in the exercise of his profession, in which this humble Christian was plainly striving to lead sinners to Christ,—in a word, to do all the good he could to all classes. There was not a servant or a child at the Springs that did not receive some kind word or token; and even the Irish laborers on the road, and in the fields around, looked for his daily greeting. Into every sick-room his influence penetrated. Among the guests was a wretched man, debased by intemperance, confined to his bed—an object of interest to no one but his physician. He was discovered by General Lee; and the Doctor said that he never loved and revered him more than when he detected his earnest and persistent efforts to raise this poor creature from the depths of degradation into which he had sunk. It was evidently not mere moral elevation at which he aimed, for in his simple and unpretending way he invariably presented the claims of the blessed Redeemer.

"I shall never forget the last visit he made to our cottage on that memorable Sabbath evening, conversing on subjects best suited to the sacred day, telling us, among other things, of his interest in colonization, in which you so deeply sympathized. He spoke of your persistent efforts to teach your slaves; and added, that when any of the servants expressed a willingness or desire to make Liberia their home, he always encouraged the inclination, provided the individuals were suitable subjects for emigration; especially felt it his duty to prepare them for the contemplated change from a home where their wants were supplied by others, to one where they would be compelled to provide for themselves; and before they were allowed to go he had them instructed in some trade suitable to their capacity. He then gave us an example of a young man who wished to go who had a talent for shoemaking, which had been encouraged by your giving him the children's shoes to mend. He first sent him to Baltimore, to be apprenticed to one of the best shoemakers in the city, to perfect him in his trade, and then to Liberia, with his wife and children, provided with all that was necessary to make him comfortable in their new home. He added that the man had prospered from the first, constantly wrote of his well-being and happiness, of the children born there, all named after members of the family; and that during the war he had manifested the deepest interest and concern in all that related personally to his former master and family."

CHAPTER XV. DAHLGREN RAID—DEATH OF GENERAL STUART.

IT was about this time (January, 1864,) that General Lee issued an order, offering a furlough to every soldier who would procure an able-bodied recruit; and several additional cavalry brigades were organized.

In the latter part of January, Richmond was endangered by a raiding party sent out by General B. F. Butler from the Peninsula. This failed in consequence of the party finding the fortification more secure than had been anticipated. It soon retreated, having lost a good many men, without the smallest compensation.

Then followed the still more threatening "Dahlgren raid." The plans for destroying the city by fire, seizing the President and Cabinet, and liberating the prisoners, were said to have been well arranged, but by the blessing of God, and the valor and arrangement of parties of our troops, they were all frustrated. Colonel Dahlgren, the leader of one of the detachments, was killed, and about eighty of his party surrendered. He was a young man of high social position, and is described as peculiarly gentle in manner and refined in sentiment and education, and scarcely over twenty years of age. It seems very sad, that so cruel a purpose should have been entrusted to one so young and highly gifted, and that he should have been the instrument to execute the evil designs of older and more violent men. Had he succeeded, the first of March would have witnessed the doom of our devoted city ; but its time was not yet; its inhabitants had much to do and to suffer before the final blow.

The night when this raiding party was so near us can never be forgotten by those persons who were in the city. It was known that the attachés of the War Department were detained there during the night; why, we knew not. About midnight brigades were seen marching up the streets; the moon shone brightly, and everybody seemed to be on the watch. The porticos and pavements were filled with ladies, as if it were in the day. Each inquired, "What is the matter?" a question which none could answer; yet every one seemed calm, quiet, and prayerful. There was no panic. Our city had often been saved as if by a miracle, and all felt I that we were in God's hands.

About two o'clock, a telegram came from General J. E. B. Stuart that he was in pursuit of the enemy. It was soon spread abroad from the War Department, and we felt safe and thankful. In a few moments the streets were deserted except by soldiers passing out, and the sentinels. Families had retired into their homes with a feeling of perfect security.

Next day General Stuart telegraphed that the enemy had been overtaken at Ashland, by Lomax's brigade, and handsomely repulsed. But on that very day, May 11th, just one year and one day after the death of General Jackson, the telegraphic wires brought the overwhelming news that our great cavalry leader, General Stuart, the Prince Rupert of the South as he has been called, had received the wound which proved to be mortal.

He was borne from the field by his staff, placed in an ambulance, and brought to Richmond with great difficulty, turning from the road and going hither and thither to avoid the enemy, every jolt inflicting the intensest agony. They at last reached the house of his brother-in-law, Doctor Brewer, in safety. But this brave young officer, the very head and front of our cavaliers, died the next day.

He had the unspeakable comfort, so often denied to the soldier, of dying among friends, with a devoted servant of God by his side, who came to administer to him the consolation of religion according to the rites of the Episcopal Church, of which he was a member, and to whom he expressed his resignation to the will of God; and soon after, having united with his feeble voice in singing "Rock of Ages, cleft for me," he quietly breathed his last.

There was one dear solace which his dying hour did not experience. His beloved wife was but fifteen miles off, but the city was so hemmed in by the enemy that she could not reach him. From time to time he turned his head to ask, "Is she come?" But she for whom his loving heart so yearned came not until that heart was stilled in death.

The President stood by him, and thanked him, in the name of the country, for his services. "I have but done my duty," was the soldier's reply.

The next evening his funeral services were performed in St. James's Church, by the Rev. Dr. Peterkin, and then his body was borne to that city of the brave and martyred dead, Hollywood Cemetery; and as the procession slowly and sorrowfully moved on,—

—the distant and random gun

That the foe was sullenly firing,

says a letter written at the time, "was his funeral knell, sounding at intervals the solemn peal, with which, in the haste and uncertainty of the time, it was impossible for us to honor him."

His death was a grievous blow to the South, and particularly to General Lee. It is said by his officers that he was plunged into the deepest grief. When the intelligence reached him, he retired from those around him, and seemed engaged in earnest prayer. He afterwards spoke of him with great feeling, saying, "I can scarcely think of him without weeping." This was a most critical time for the country, and his loss was peculiarly severe.

General Lee had from the beginning of spring fully realized the odds that were against him. The Federal Government had made immense efforts for the campaign. General Grant had become commander of the Northern myriads. The whole "Army of Northern Virginia" did not exceed fifty thousand men, and there was no immediate hope of reinforcements. Then our Christian warrior turned to the Lord of Hosts for help in his weakness, and issued a General Order, recommending Friday, the 8th of April, as a day of fasting, humiliation, and prayer. He invited the army to join in the observance of the day. Chaplains wire ordered to hold services in their regiments and brigades, and the officers and men were requested to attend. He concluded the order with these words:

Soldiers! let us humble ourselves before Almighty God, asking, through Christ, the forgiveness of our sins, beseeching the aid of the God of our forefathers in the defence of our homes and our liberties, thanking Him for His past blessings, and imploring their continuance upon our cause and people.

In the beginning of this campaign of 1864, the great importance of it was deeply impressed on the minds of the people. Wives, mothers, and sisters worked and prayed for their stricken country; earnest were their exhortations to their loved ones to be true to their country and the glorious cause. The veterans of Lee were inspired by patriotism, and buckled on their armor with determined hands for the coming conflict. The battle was not yet to the strong.

On the 5th and 6th of May was fought and won the desperate battle of "The Wilderness." The same entangled wilderness which had been the field of victory the year before, where the forests were so thick that it was impossible for a regimental commander to see the whole of his line at once. General Lee had chosen his own ground, and his troops had the advantage of a thorough acquaintance with the country. Generals A, P. Hill, Longstreet, Ewell, Gordon,

Kershaw, and other general officers, took part in this glorious victory. Here the gallant Gen. Jenkins, of South Carolina, was mortally wounded by a party of our own men, and Gen. Longstreet received a severe wound in his throat from the same party.

The next day Gen. Grant took up the line of march for Spottsylvania Court-House, hoping to place himself between Lee and Richmond. In this attempt he was foiled by General Lee's having seen through the plan, and having ordered Longstreet's corps, now commanded by General Anderson, to march to that place, where he was soon followed by the whole army.

On the morning of the 9th both armies were concentrated—the Confederates on the southern bank of the river Po, the Federals on the northern. The fighting was desperate on both sides for three days, without great advantages to either. It was during this time, and in connection with the movement on Spottsylvania Court-House, that Sheridan sent out raiding parties towards Richmond, which parties acted in concert with those already mentioned.

Now General Lee began that wonderful retreat, said to be the most masterly on record, from the Rappahannock to the James, fighting ah occasion required, with more or less success, but keeping General Grant at bay.

On the 5th of June occurred the decisive battle of Cold Harbor, in Hanover County, which closed the campaign, leaving General Grant again foiled.

"During these critical days," says John E. Cooke, in his excellent biography of General Lee, himself an eye-witness, "General Lee acted with the nerve and coolness of a soldier, whom no adverse event can shake. Those who saw him will testify to the stern courage of his expression; the glance of the eye, which indicated a great nature aroused to the depth of its powerful organization."

On one occasion, at the battle of Spottsylvania Court-House, he witnessed a scene too characteristic of the devotion of men and officers to their leader to be omitted.

Lee was on fire with the ardor of battle, which so seldom mastered him. He went forward in front of his line, and taking his station beside the colors of one of his Virginia regiments, took off his hat, and, turning to the men, pointed towards the enemy. A storm of cheers greeted the General as he sat on his gray war-horse ill front of the men, his head bare, his eye flashing, and his cheek flushed with the fighting-blood of the soldier. General Gordon spurred to his side, and seized his rein. "General Lee!" he exclaimed, "this is no place for you. Go to the rear. These are Virginians and Georgians, sir,—men who have never failed! Men, you will not fail now!" he cried, rising in his stirrups and addressing the troops.

"No, no!" was the reply of the men; and from the whole line burst the shout, "Lee to the rear! Lee to the rear!" Instead of being needed, it was obvious that his presence was an embarrassment, as the men seemed determined not to charge unless he retired. He accordingly did so; and the line advanced, led by General Gordon, who was never so happy as when the air around him was filled with bullets.

Three days after the battle of Cold Harbor, General Grant determined to retire south of the James and besiege Richmond from that direction. In the retreat from the Rappahannock, he had lost twenty men to Lee's one; but the depletion in the Southern army, though comparatively small, could not be repaired. The South had done her best—men and means were exhausted. The soldiers in the field were veterans. The courage of rank and file was wonderful; hope still filled the soldiers' breasts. The people, too, never yielded to despair. Sheridan and Hunter had spread ruin through the beautiful valley of Virginia. "Over two thousand barns filled with wheat, hay, and farming utensils had been destroyed; seventy mills with grain burned." This quotation is from Sheridan's dispatch, of which one of their own historians says, "This dread bulletin recites acts some of which are indefensible."

From this time, during the summer and autumn of 1864, hostilities continued with varied success. The soldiers looked to General Lee as to one inspired; he was the hope of the country, and all prayed for his safety, feeling that the weapon that should end his life would also end the life of the beloved Confederacy. He must have known that the cause was almost hopeless; and yet, with a firm and calm reliance upon Providence, he never for a moment wavered in his duty to his country. Remembering his great maxim, that "Human virtue should be equal to human calamity," he seemed never to lose his "heart of hope." "For myself," said he to one of the Senators, "I intend to die sword in hand;" but God had willed it otherwise, and reserved His great Christian soldier to set an example of pure and undefiled religion amid the peaceful shades of civil life.

During this winter the Confederate Congress appointed him Commander-in-chief of the armies of the Confederacy, with was confirmed by the Executive on the same day, He accepted the appointment with his usual modesty, and then issued a characteristic General Order, invoking the guidance of Almighty God, and expressing his reliance upon the courage and fortitude of the troops, sustained by the and firmness of the people, feeling confidence that their united efforts, under the blessing of Heaven, would secure peace and independence.

A Northern editor at that time, commenting on his appointment and the evacuation of Charleston, says, "It has been said that the rebellion was a shell. The shell is ours; and while we hold the worthless fragments, its invulnerable core—the great strong heart—defies and baffles us. To one who truly conceives the meaning of the change of policy that has been inaugurated by the abandonment of Charleston, the shadow of coming battles looks darker and more vast than ever before. To one brain, we know how fertile the resources; to one heart, we know how firm and tree; to one intellect, we know how gifted with martial attributes; to one man, we know how capable to plan, to strike, to retrieve error, or to take advantage of it, the military fortunes of the South have been confided." Such was the opinion of the Northern press of our great commander. The North evidently feared a plan, which General Lee had hoped to carry out, of uniting the armies, and carrying the war farther South; but it little knew how entirely gone were our resources.

CHAPTER XVI. LEE APPOINTED COMMANDER-IN-CHIEF— SUFFERINGS OF THE TROOPS.

THE appointment of General Lee renewed the hope of the people and the army, and, notwithstanding the sufferings of the soldiers, they were bright and cheerful; and it is difficult to conceive how they maintained their lightness of spirits. Our forefathers in the old Revolution had their hardships. The winter at Valley Forge could hardly be surpassed; but their sorrows were personal. There was no poignant anxiety for the loved ones at home, many of them surrounded by the enemy. They knew that, and knew nothing more, for there could be no communication; others knew that their families were subjected to the most galling poverty, in a devastated country; still these ragged, half-starved patriots suffered, and did what they could for their country.

John E. Cooke gives a graphic account of the army to which he belonged, and, as an eye-witness, he could not be mistaken, nor is the picture overdrawn.

"The condition of the army," he says, "in which 'companies' scarce existed, 'regiments' were counted by tens, and 'divisions' by hundreds only, need not here be elaborately dwelt upon. It was indeed the phantom of an army, and the gaunt faces were almost ghostly. Shoeless, in rags, with just sufficient coarse food to sustain life, but never enough to keep at arm's length the gnawing fiend Hunger, Lee's old veterans remained firm, scattered like a thin skirmish-line along forty miles of works; while opposite to them lay an enemy in the highest state of efficiency, and numbering nearly five men to their one. That the soldiers of the army retained their nerve under circumstances so discouraging is surely an honorable fact, and will make their names glorious in history. They remained unshaken and fought undismayed to the last, although their courage was subjected to trials of the most exhausting character. Day and night, from month to month, the incessant fire of the Federal forces had continued, and every engine of human destruction had been put in play to wear away their strength. They fought all through the cheerless days of winter, and when they lay down in the cold trenches at eight, the shell of the Federal mortars rained down upon them, bursting and mortally wounding them. All day long the fire of muskets and cannon, and then from sunset to dawn the curving fire of the roaring mortars, and the steady, never-ceasing crack of the sharp-shooters along the front. Snow, or blinding sleet, or freezing rains might be falling, but the fire went on,—it seemed destined to go on to all eternity."*

Still they kept up their spirits, and the younger portion of them amused themselves at their own sufferings, and with the proverbial recklessness of the camp seemed joyous amid starvation. They called themselves "Lee's Miserables."

The sprightly authoress of the "Popular Life of Lee" gives the following account of the origin of the name. "Victor Hugo's work, Les Misérables, had been translated and published by a house in Richmond; the soldiers, in the great dearth of reading-matter, had seized upon it; and thus, by a strange chance, the tragic story of the great French writer had become known to the soldiers in the trenches. Everywhere you might see the gaunt figures in their tattered jackets, bending over the dingy pamphlets—'Fantine,' 'Cosette,' 'Marius,' or 'St. Denis,' and the woes of 'Jean Valjean,' the old galley-slave, found an echo in the hearts of these brave soldiers, immured in the trenches and fettered by duty to their muskets or their cannon."

A story went the rounds of the newspapers at this time, of an old woman, who, seeing the notice of one of this series in a bookseller's shop, "Les Misérables," "Fantine," mistook it for a bulletin from the seat of war. "Lee's Miserables, fainting!" exclaimed the excited old lady, and she went in to ask for further details, as her son was one of them.

There was no bound to the love of the soldiers for their commander. They knew that he did all he could to ameliorate their condition; that he suffered with them, and enjoyed no luxuries. Richmond continued to send out her supplies, and the surrounding country—depleted, overrun, and hemmed in as it was—did its best for them. But little could be drawn from the lands. The flourishing wheat-field of to-day would probably be grazed by the cavalry of the enemy to-morrow, and the laden wagon for the commissariat might be, nay, probably would be, the prey of the raiding party.

The scarcity of provisions in Richmond during this winter may be better understood by a little circumstance which came under the writer's eye, and which formed a striking exemplification of the efficacy of prayer offered in faith, nothing doubting.

A chaplain in the Confederate service—a refugee from his home—received a letter from the noble-hearted Mr. J. R. Bryan, of Fluvanna County, telling him that he had deposited with a commission merchant nineteen hams of bacon, subject to his order, to be given to the same number of refugees to whom he thought a ham would be acceptable.

The chaplain's wife had that evening called to see a lady belonging to one of the most influential families in Virginia. She had not lived in her native State for many years before the war; and her five sons were engaged in their several avocations, north of her borders: but, when they knew that their beloved South was in danger, they, with one accord, followed the example of their great chief, left all and came to her assistance. The widowed mother gave up her comfortable home, followed her sons, and sought a support by writing in one of the Government offices. She was now suffering from the absence of those sons, exposed to danger and death, as they were ill the several branches of the army. One only was not now fighting for his country, and he had been for many months a prisoner at Fort Delaware. She poured into her friend's sympathetic ear the causes of her anxiety, but not a complaint escaped her; though it was evident that her share of the depreciated currency paid for her services was scarcely adequate to her support.

The lady returned to her lodgings, and her husband immediately handed her Mr. B.'s letter, with the request that she would assist him in finding out the roost needy among their refugee acquaintances. Their name was legion; and the list was easily and joyfully made out, at the head of it was the friend of the evening. The necessary order for the ham was written and carefully laid aside, to be taken to her early in the morning.

On kindly thoughts intent, the lady arose with the early dawn to take the order to her friend, and was shocked to find that the streets were covered with sleet, and the snow was falling rapidly. After the first feeling of disappointment, she determined, reluctantly, to wait until the weather was more propitious. The doubt then arose in her mind about the propriety of doing so. The inclement day might have found her friend totally unprepared for it, and alone. Was it right to prevent her having meat to-day—to withhold from her any comfort which it was in her power to bestow? The argument went on in her own mind, and after an animated discussion between sympathy and prudence, her husband, who was too sick to take her place, was called into the council. He agreed with sympathy, that the friend should have the ham at once, but with prudence, that his wife should not expose herself to such weather. Finally sympathy triumphed, and the lady, with overshoes, cloak, and umbrella, set off on her slippery and somewhat dangerous walk of love. The middle of the street, where the way was rough, could only be trodden with safety. The house was reached, the icy door-steps were passed in safety; then up two flights of stairs, and the tap at the door was answered by a fine-looking young officer in colonel's uniform. He was at once recognized as the son, from his long incarceration at Fort Delaware. The breakfast-table was arranged for two—with snowy napkins, bright silver, and pretty china, the remnants of former days.

The recognition and congratulations being over, the mother was summoned to the passage, and the "order" given to her. For a moment she uttered not a word; tears streamed, and her eyes were lifted to heaven. "The gift of God," she at last exclaimed.

Mr. Bryan is good; your husband is good; you are good to come out in such weather; but you are all sent by God. My son came unexpectedly last night, at a late hour, worn and weary. My heart overflowed with gratitude and joy. I had tea, bread and butter for him; nothing more. After his long imprisonment and hardship, I had no meat for him, and no hope of getting it. I did not tell him so, but I told God, and asked him to help me. After my fervent prayer I went to sleep peacefully, thankful that my child was with me again safe and well; but in the dark hours of the night I awoke, and the troubled thought came over me, "How can I make him comfortable for the few days he will be with me, before he returns to the army." I arose and knelt at my bedside, and besought God to give me food for my son. I saw no probability of it, and yet I hoped that He would see fit to grant my prayer; and He has done it, blessed be His name.

At this time, it must be remembered, many of the inhabitants of Richmond, even those who had been most accustomed to lives of ease and elegance, had no luxuries; then how much more was it the case with those persons, particularly ladies, who had necessarily left their homes and sought the Capital as the place where they might gain the means of living by working for the Government. They worked cheerfully and hopefully, and privations were not regarded as such.

Notes

* Cooke's Life of General Lee.

CHAPTER XVII. THE FALL OF RICHMOND, AND THE SURRENDER.

THE early spring of 1865 dawned on a declining cause, but still hopeful people; but the Confederacy was doomed. The greatest military genius in America, as General Scott most justly called General Lee, had led brave men who fought for home and country against overpowering numbers of veteran troops, and had led them to victory; but no human power could avert the calamities which now overshadowed the devoted South. Men who would never succumb to the missiles of war must now yield to grim want. Time wore on, and too soon came the end. The heart-rending surrender of Richmond on the 3d of April, and the final surrender on the 9th, are events too sad to dwell upon, but for the picture they present of a great Christian warrior mighty in defeat. Richmond had for months known herself to be in a state of siege. She knew that the serpent, wonderful for size and wiliness, was wrapping her in its coils, only waiting for the moment when he might strike his fangs into her heart, or crush her in its embrace. Yet was she calm, busily engaged as her men and women were in doing their duty to their country. They never for a moment allowed themselves to despair; they knew that they were in God's hand, and that He was working by instruments, to which they were willing to trust themselves. They did not dream of failure.

The morning sun of the 2d of April arose brightly on a peaceful city; the church-bells which had not been cast into cannon, at eleven o'clock summoned the multitudes to their various places of worship. Friend passed friend on the street with the usual salutation of kindness, until the churches were filled with their congregations.

In the Episcopal churches, as usual on the first Sunday of the month, the sacrament of the Lord's Supper was administered. The President was at St. Paul's. The services were nearly over, when a messenger entered, and handed him a paper. It was General Lee's dispatch announcing his determination to evacuate the city. The President's agitation alarmed a portion of the congregation; in a few moments the blessing was pronounced, and all left the church,— many in alarm, all agitated by uncertainty. At St. James's Church, Adjutant-General Cooper occupied his usual seat. As he was about to leave it to approach the Lord's Table, a messenger walked quickly down the aisle, and extended his hand to give him a paper; but he was too much absorbed by the sacred rite to observe it. A gentleman sitting by received the dispatch, and held it until the venerable Christian returned to his seat, and then placed it in his hand. His cheek blanched as he read it, and he quietly left the church. All this passed as the communicants were passing to and fro in the aisles, and therefore it was observed but by a few persons, and they were too deeply anxious to communicate their feelings to others; but the moment soon came, when the congregation left the church and mingled with the thousands of anxious citizens who were moving in the streets. Horror and despair marked every countenance—some, agitated arid excited, expressed their feelings of woe, other went on in pallid silence. Some were rushing in pursuit of vehicles to carry them out of the city, they knew not whither; others, who were obliged to remain in the city, seemed to be calmly resigning themselves to the hands of God; the more sanguine men, still sending forth rays of hope, saying decidedly and confidently, "General Lee knows what he is about; he will remove the army farther south, where provisions are more abundant. The President will take the

Government off, and re-establish it in some Southern town, and it will not be long before we are disenthralled. Nothing better could happen for the Confederacy, &c." These were pleasant words, and we loved to hear them; but we listened to them with a strange, unrealizing feeling.

That night was passed, we scarcely know how; no one slept: the explosion of magazines, again and again, shook the houses and shivered the windows with a crashing sound. All was wild confusion. By daybreak it was discovered that the lower parts of the city were in flames; large commissary and quartermaster buildings were most unwisely fired, as well as some of the tobacco factories; and the flames spread from street to street,—in a few hours the principal business streets, the War Department, and other fine buildings presented a mass of blackened ruins. The armory was filled with bomb-shells, which exploded from time to time as the fire reached them, resembling heavy cannonading.

The Federal troops entered the city at an early hour. They treated the citizens with great courtesy, but the situation was humiliating in the extreme. But where was our great Chief from whom we still expected so much? His family remained in Richmond, but he was drawing off his army from Richmond and Petersburg under cover of darkness. A brave member of his staff dashed into the city at midnight, went to the house of a friend with whom his lady-love was refugeeing, claimed her promise to marry him if the city was evacuated; summoned a clergyman and a few friends, was married, placed his bride under his mother's care, and was again with the army by break of day.

It is said that the soldiers were in fine spirits, hoping to go South and fight on. General Lee, too, was hopeful. "I have gotten my army safe out of the breastworks," he was heard to say; "and in order to follow me, the enemy must abandon his lines, and can derive no farther benefit from the railroads and James River."

General Lee designed taking his army into North Carolina, but the question of food, the very means of subsistence, was now the important one. The army had carried but one ration. Orders had been given for a supply to meet him at Amelia Court-House. By some fatal mistake, the cars laden with food from the South were sent on to Richmond without unloading at that point, and the provisions were lost in the general conflagration. The army had marched through mud and water, delayed by the risen streams which they must cross, buoyed by the hope that relief was near. What, then, must have been their bitter disappointment, when they reached the desired haven, to find that all hope was fallacious! How must the great heart of General Lee have quailed at the unlooked-for calamity! Starving men could neither march nor fight. It became necessary to send out foraging parties to gain a scanty subsistence from the impoverished country through which they passed. Next day his retreat was cut off while the troops were out hunting for bread. General Lee was then obliged to turn to the westward and retreat towards Lynchburg. The army of Northern Virginia marched on unmurmuringly, confident of the ability of their leader in any extremity.

The Federals under General Sheridan hung on the flank of the army. On the 6th a sharp fight ensued, in which the Confederates under General Ewell, though so overcome with fatigue as in many instances to fall asleep at their guns, held their ground for some time, keeping the enemy at bay by an overwhelming fire; but the enemy being largely reinforced, General Ewell found himself obliged to surrender, This blow was irreparable. General Ewell and nearly his whole corps, with several general officers, were now in the hands of the enemy. This occurrence took place while General Lee was confronting a body of Federals near Sailor's Creek.

"The scene," says one who witnessed it, "was one of gloomy picturesqueness and tragic interest. On a plateau raised above the forest from which they had emerged were the disorganized troops of Ewell and Anderson, unofficered, and uttering exclamations of rage and defiance. Rising above the weary groups which had thrown themselves upon the ground were the grim barrels of cannon in battery, ready to fire as soon as the enemy appeared. In front of all was placed the still line of battle, placed by General Lee, and waiting calmly. Lee had rushed his infantry over just at sunset, leading it in person, his face animated and his eye brilliant with the soldier's spirit of fight, but his bearing unflurried as before. An artist desiring his picture ought to have seen the old cavalier at this moment, sweeping on upon his large iron-gray, whose mane and tail floated in the wind; carrying his field-glass half raised in his right hand, with head erect, gestures animated, and in the whole face and form the expression of the hunter close upon his game. The line once interposed, he rode in the twilight among the disordered groups above mentioned, and the sight of him aroused a tumult. Fierce cries resounded on all sides, and, with hands clinched violently and raised aloft, the men called on him to lead them against the enemy. 'It's General Lee! Uncle Robert! Where's the man who won't follow Uncle Robert?' I heard on all sides; the swarthy faces, full of dirt and courage, lit up every instant by the glare of the burning wagons. Altogether, the scene was indescribable."*

On the 7th, General Fitz-Lee gave an unexpected repulse to a cavalry force under General Sheridan. Again General Fitz-Lee met and captured a force of about six thousand. General Lee was very much gratified, and said to his son, General Wm. H. F. Lee:

"Keep your command together, and in good spirits, General. Don't let them think of surrender. I will get you out of this."

On the 8th and 9th hope seemed to die in the breast of every human being except the Commanding General. The resolution of the troops, in consequence of hunger and other hardships incident to retreat, seemed to waver. The men were almost without food, except a little corn; but those who were still able to carry their muskets, marched and fought with wonderfal cheerfulness.

General Lee's spirits did not flag, and up to the last day he did not seriously contemplate surrender. The corps commanders first saw the necessity, and requested General Pendleton, his chief of artillery, to suggest to General Lee the hopelessness of a longer struggle. The communication came like a shock.

"Surrender!" he exclaimed, his eyes flashing. "I have too many good fighting-men for that."*

On the night of the 8th, the last council of war of the army of Northern Virginia was held. It met around a bivouac-fire in the woods. General Lee, Generals Gordon, Longstreet, and Fitz-Lee were present. Generals Gordon and Fitz-Lee half reclined upon an army blanket near the fire. Longstreet sat upon a log smoking, and General Lee stood by the fire, holding in his hand the correspondence which had just passed between Grant and himself. The question was course it was advisable to pursue, was put by General Lee in a calm voice. It was agreed that the army should advance on the next morning beyond Appomattox Court-House, and if only General Sheridan's cavalry was in front to brush it from the path and proceed to Lynchburg. If, however, the Federal cavalry vas discovered in large force, then to dispatch a flag to General Grant, requesting an interview to arrange terms of capitulation. General Lee acquiesced in the plan with such deep heart-burning as none will ever know.

At three o'clock in the morning he awoke from his troubled sleep by the bivouac-fire, and sent Colonel Venable to know General Gordon's opinion as to the probable result of another attack upon the army. The answer was most discouraging. He received it with great feeling, and said:

"There is nothing left but to go to General Grant; and I had rather die a thousand deaths."

One of his staff officers said to him. "What will history say of our surrendering, if there is any chance of escape? Posterity will not understand it!"

General Lee immediately replied, "Yes, yes, they will understand our situation; but that is not the question. The question is, 'What is right?' If it is right, I take the responsibility!"

His expression now changed from hopefulness to deep melancholy, and turning to an officer near, he said, "How easily I could get rid of all this and be at rest! I have only to ride along the line and all would be over." He was silent for a short time, and then added, with a deep sigh, "But it is our duty to live. What will become of the women and children of the South, if we are not here to protect them?"

Further resistance seeming impossible, General Lee sent a flag to General Grant, requesting an interview, that the terms of surrender might, if possible, be arranged. This meeting took place at the house of Mr. Wilmer McLean, at Appomattox Court-House. General Lee vas accompanied by his aid, Colonel Marshall; General Grant by a few of his officers. He (General Grant;) behaved with great courtesy and delicacy. The demeanor of General Lee was as usual, that which marked the Christian gentleman, calm and courteous, 2nd he confined his remarks strictly to the bitter business before him.

The interview was brief. Seated at a plain deal table, the two commanders wrote and exchanged the necessary papers. They then bowed to each other, and leaving the house, General Lee mounted his gray war-horse and returned to his headquarters. As he passed through the army the men gathered around him, and with love and sorrow called upon God to help him. He was deeply afflicted; tears came to his eyes as he said in tremulous tones, "We have fought through the war together. I have done the best I could for you. My heart is too full to say more." He then passed into his tent, where he was left by his considerate officers to commune with his own heart and with his God. His appearance on that day is thus described by a Federal officer:

General Lee looked very much jaded and worn, but nevertheless presented the same magnificent physique for which he has always been noted. He was neatly dressed in gray cloth, without embroidery or any insignia of rank, except three stars worn on the turned portion of his collar. His cheeks were very much bronzed by exposure, but still shone ruddy beneath it all. He is growing quite bald, and wears one of the side-locks of his hair thrown across the upper portion of his forehead, which is as white and fair as a woman's. He stands fully six feet in height, and weighs something over two hundred pounds, without being burdened with a pound of superfluous flesh. During the interview he was retired and dignified to a degree bordering on taciturnity, but was free from all exhibition of temper or mortification. His demeanor was that of a thoroughly possessed gentleman who had a very disagreeable duty to perform, but was determined to get through it as well and as soon as possible.

On the day after the capitulation, General Lee issued the following farewell address to his old soldiers:

HEADQUARTERS ARMY OF NORTHERN VIRGINIA,

April 10, 1865.

GENERAL ORDER, No. 9.

VETERANS OF THE ARMY OF NORTHERN VIRGINIA: After four years of arduous service, marked by unsurpassed courage and fortitude, the army of Northern Virginia has been compelled to yield to overwhelming numbers and resources.

I need not tell the survivors of so many hard-fought battles, who have remained steadfast to the last, that I have consented to this result from no distrust of them; but, feeling that valor and devotion could accomplish nothing that could compensate for the loss that would have attended the continuation of the contest, I have determined to avoid the useless sacrifice of those whose past services have endeared them to their countrymen.

By the terms of agreement, officers and men can return to their homes and remain there until exchanged.

You will take with you the satisfaction that proceeds from the consciousness of duty faithfully performed; and I earnestly pray that a merciful God will extend to you His blessing and protection.

With an unceasing admiration of your constancy and devotion to your country, and a grateful remembrance of your kindness and generous consideration of myself, I bid you, soldiers, an affectionate farewell.

R. E. LEE, General.

On the 12th of April the army of Northern Virginia made their last sad march to Appomattox Court-House, and laid down the arms which they had never dishonored, and the flags which had floated over heroes as brave, and battle-fields as gloriously contested, as ancient or modern history can boast.

The victors were kind and considerate of the feelings of our vanquished heroes. Neither music nor cheers were heard, except distant music from those who were not aware of what was passing, and that was apologized for by one of the officers. But the heart of the South was broken; the sword of Robert Lee was sheathed forever.

The sadness of that thought called forth from our gifted Southern poet, "Father Ryan," the following touching lines:

THE SWORD OF LEE.

Forth from its scabbard, pure and bright,
　　Flashed forth the sword of Lee!
For in the front of the deadly fight,
High o'er the brave, in the cause of right,
Its stainless sheen, like a beacon light,
　　Led us to victory.
Out of its scabbard, where full long
　　It slumbered peacefully—
Roused from its rest by the battle-song,
Shielding the feeble, smiting the strong,
Guarding the right, and avenging the wrong—
　　Gleamed the sword of Lee!
Forth from the scabbard, high in air,
　　Beneath Virginia's sky;
And they who saw it gleaming there.
And knew who bore it, knelt to swear
That where that sword led they would dare
　　To follow and to die.
Out of its scabbard! Never hand

Waved sword from stain so free,
Nor purer sword led braver band,
Nor braver bled for a brighter land,
Nor brighter land had a cause as grand,
   Never cause a chief like Lee!
Forth from the scabbard! how we prayed
   That sword might victor be!
And when our triumph was delayed,
And many a heart grew sore afraid,
We still hoped on, while gleamed the blade
   Of noble Robert Lee!
Forth from its scabbard! all in vain!
   Forth flashed the sword of Lee!
'Tis shrouded now in its sheath again;
It sleeps the sleep of our noble slain,
Defeated, yet without a stain,
   Proudly and peacefully.

The painful arrangements being over, General Lee set out for Richmond, like his men, a paroled prisoner. The parting from the soldiers was most pathetic. He pressed the hand of each man who stood near enough; uttered a farewell which can be better imagined than described; mounted his noble "Traveller," and slowly left the scene of his deep mortification. Accompanied by a party of about twenty-five horsemen, among whom was a detachment of Federal cavalry, he turned his face towards Richmond. Among the wagons carrying the private effects of the party was the well-known old black vehicle which he had occasionally used during the war when too unwell to travel on horseback. He had also been in the habit of carrying stores for the wounded, but had never used it for transporting articles for his own convenience.*

During the ride, the impoverished people watched for him, to welcome him with demonstrations of affection and admiration. They had provisions prepared for him, and were gratified to have him under their roofs, and to give anything, everything, for his comfort. He gratified them by most graciously accepting their kindness; but said to one of his officers, "These people are kind, too kind. Their hearts are as full as when we began our first campaign in 1861. They do too much, for they cannot now afford it."

He seemed unwilling to give up his soldierly habits, for when d poor woman, at whose house he stopped, showed him a nice bed she had prepared for him, he courteously declined, and, spreading his blanket down, he slept on the floor. He was evidently unwilling to enjoy comforts which the gentlemen who accompanied him could not share.

Notes

* Cooke's Life of General Lee.

* J. E. Cooke.

* J. E. Cooke.

CHAPTER XVIII. LEE RETURNS TO RICHMOND.

WHEN within a mile or two of Richmond he rode ahead of his escort, only accompanied by a few officers. Mayo's bridge had been destroyed when the Confederates retreated, but crossing a pontoon bridge placed there by the Federals, he crossed into Richmond,—sad, enthralled Richmond, enslaved and in ruins. What a sorrowful sight to him, as he rode through the masses of rubbish in the burnt district, which reached nearly to the residence of his family. Cary and Main Streets, and large portions of others were in ruins.

As soon as he was recognized, the intelligence spread from lip to lip that General Lee had come. The inhabitants rushed from their homes to welcome him; the streets re-echoed with cheers and shouts, and were gay once more with waving handkerchiefs and other demonstrations of welcome. He wished to avoid this outpouring of feeling. He raised his hat and courteously bowed, but rode on in silence to his own home, where his wife and children awaited him. When he entered the house, the crowd silently withdrew; no one intruded on his privacy. The circumstances were too painful, and the very rabble respected his desire to be alone with his family.

The following entry is in the diary of a gentleman then in Richmond.

General Lee is in Richmond. He came without parade, but could n't come unobserved. As soon as his appearance was whispered about, a crowd gathered in his path, not boisterously, but respectfully, and thickening rapidly as he advanced to his house on Franklin Street, between 8th and 9th, when, with a courtly bow to the multitude, he at once retired to the bosom of his own beloved family. How universal and profound is the respect felt for this great commander, though returning from defeat and disaster! He had done all that could be accomplished with the means placed under his control, all that skill and valor could do. The scenes of the surrender were noble and touching beyond the power of language to describe. General Grant's bearing was profoundly respectful; General Lee's courtly and lofty as the purest chivalry could require. The terms, so honorable to all parties, being complied with to the letter, our arms were laid down with breaking hears and tears such as sternest warriors may shed! "Woe worth the day."

All over now! The trumpet-blast,
  The hurried trampling to and fro,
The sky with battle-smoke o'ercast,
  The flood of death and woe,
All ended now. The siren song
  Of Hope's ecstatic lay is hushed;
And minor chords, in plaintive tones,
  Wail out where gayer notes are crushed.
'Neath feathery snow, in hallowed ground,
  By far Potomac's rippling stream
Our loved ones sleep; the lulling waves
  Can ne'er disturb the soldier's dream.
They whisper, "Peace,"—the dove of peace,

Like Noah's, searches for her nest;
She folds her wings among the dead,
    But with the living finds no rest.
All over now! We gave our all—
    Our loved ones, homes, and prayers;
God wills that we awhile shall wait,
    In bitterness and tears.
What need of tears? Why must they flow,
    When all but life and breath are gone?
God help us all! and help the heart
    To murmur still, "Thy will be done!"

CHAPTER XIX. THE LOVE OF HIS SOLDIERS.

NONE who were in Richmond after General Lee's return thither, can forget how eagerly the citizens availed themselves of every opportunity to do him homage. How they loved him; how their hearts mingled with his in sympathy and sorrow; how they felt the "union and communion of hearts that had been fused by tribulation." In the hour of success, they had almost idolized him; now they had the sweeter feeling of a love which was purified by suffering. The Northern tourists, who came with hast to see the rebel city which had given them so much trouble, now clustered about the door to see the man whom they had feared, but now honored because of his moral grandeur in adversity. He received most courteously a deputation of Federal officers who had come to show their appreciation of his character and their good feelings towards him. But the expressions of affection which had gratified him more than any others, were those of his soldiers. These soldiers, who were now constantly returning from the Northern prisons, all ragged and dirty as they were, could not, they said, return to their ruined homes without once more seeing their beloved commander.

General Lee often said that those interviews gave him great pain, but he could not avoid them, without "wounding the feelings of those warm-hearted soldiers."

One day he was called down to see two old soldiers, who advanced towards him with the military salute, and immediately told him that they were sent by "some fellows round the corner," who were too badly dressed to come before him. They had just returned from prison. "Come, go with us," they begged, "and a whole army can't take you from us. We want to take care of you. They have captured our President, and they threaten you. Come to our mountains, where we will die in your defence."

"But," answered the General, "you would not have your General run away and hide himself. He must stay and meet his fate."

He then explained to them that the terms of the surrender ensured his safety, and that he relied on General Grant's word. He could, however, with difficulty, dissuade them from their generous purpose. He then insisted upon their accepting two suits of his own clothes, as he had nothing else to offer in memory of him, and as an assurance of his gratitude for their disinterested love for him, They pressed the clothes to their lips with warmth, and then returned to their comrades to tell them the result of their mission, and to exhibit their prize. Who can doubt that those clothes are treasured up, to be handed down to their children's children, as a most precious legacy.

Miss Mason, in her "Poplar Life of Lee," relates one other well-authenticated anecdote, showing the love with which he inspired the plainest of his soldiers.

A warm-hearted Irishman, one day, appeared at his door, and being told that the General was busy writing, and wished to be excused, replied, "I know he is busy: I will detain him but one moment, I only want to take him by the hand." At this moment, the General, who was passing through the hall, heard these words, and came forward, offering his hand, which was grasped with intense emotion. "I have come all the way from Baltimore to take your hand. I have three sons born during the war—Beauregard, Fitz-Lee, and Robert Lee. My wife would never forgive me if I should go home without seeing you. God bless you!" And with this outburst he departed.

It is said by those who knew him best, that even while suffering most from the mortification of defeat, he never expressed one word of bitterness against the North, but always set an example of moderation and Christian forbearance, and tried to reconcile others to their fate by bearing his own with equanimity, and even cheerfulness. Many young men, in the bitterness of their disappointment, wished to leave the country. This he always discouraged, and advised them to stay at home, and heal the wounds from which the South was suffering. During the war, he never allowed a word of harshness towards the enemy, without rebuking it by example or word.

After the battle of Spottsylvania Court-House, one of his Generals standing near, looked towards the Federal army, and in bitterness of spirit said, with a scowl, "I wish they were all dead!"

General Lee immediately turned to him and said, with his benevolent smile, "How can you say that, General? I wish they were at home attending to their business, and leaving us to do the same. Let us wish them nothing worse."

It was this feeling of the purest Christianity which enabled him during the war to resist the appeals made to him to adopt measures of retaliation. Thus, in the hostile portions of Maryland, and in Pennsylvania, when the men longed to turn their horses on the rich fields of grain, and to refresh themselves by forcibly partaking of the good things which were around them in the most tempting abundance, or, as one of the men expressed it, "Just to apply the fagot to one house, to pay for the one burned over the head of my wife and children on the Mississippi," their General would reply, "No; if I suffer my army to pursue such a course, I cannot invoke the blessing of God on my arms."

Forgiveness of enemies seems to have been a principle so deeply interwoven with his life as to become a part of his purified nature. This was peculiarly exemplified when a gentleman called upon him, at the request of a Federal officer, to communicate to him that he had been, or would be, indicted in the United States Court at Norfolk for treason. The gentleman could not resist the impulse to express his indignation at such conduct in our oppressors. As he was about to take his leave, General Lee arose, took his hand, and said, with a gracious smile and most kindly tones, "We must forgive our enemies, I can truly say, that not a day has passed since the war began that I have not prayed for them."

The same spirit induced him to rebuke gently a lady who, having been made a widow by the war, brought her two sons to Washington College to put them under General Lee's care. In alluding to the past, she expressed herself with great bitterness towards the North. General Lee, with a sympathetic voice, replied, "Madam, do not bring up your sons in hostility to the United States. Remember, we are one country now. Dismiss from your mind all sectional feeling, and bring your children up Americans."

That he would share his substance with them is attested by a citizen of the North, who thus describes an interview with him.

One day, last summer, I saw General Lee standing at his gate, talking pleasantly to an humbly clad man, who seemed very much pleased at, the cordial courtesy of the great chieftain, and turned off evidently delighted as we came up. After exchanging salutations, the General said, pointing to the retreating form, "That is one of our old soldiers in necessitous circumstances." I took it for granted that it was some veteran Confederate, when the noble-minded chieftain quietly added, "He fought on the other side; but we must not think of that." I afterwards ascertained, not from General Lee,—for he never alluded to his charities,—that he had not only spoken kindly to this old soldier "who had fought on the other side," but he had sent him on his way rejoicing in a liberal contribution to his necessities.

While President of Washington College, General Lee was present, one night, when a party of gentlemen were discussing some recent legislation of Congress on Southern affairs. They spoke with indignation and bitterness of the unjust and ungenerous treatment of the South. He remained silent; but when the conversation was over, wrote the following lines upon a slip of paper and handed them to the gentlemen, saying, "If a heathen poet could write in this way, what should be the feeling of a Christian?"

Learn from yon orient shell to love thy foe,
And store with pearls the hand that brings thee woe.
Free, like yon rock, from base, vindictive pride,
Emblaze with gems the wrist that rends thy side.
Mark, where yon tree rewards the stony shower
With fruit nectareous or the balmy flower.
All nature cries aloud, "Shall man do less
Than heal the smiter, and the railer bless?"*

General Lee had offered his all to his country—his life, his sons, his fortune, his home; but, now that his mighty efforts had proved unavailing, with a Christian spirit rarely attained by mortal mail, he bowed to the decree of his heavenly Father, and set an example to his countrymen of forbearance and forgiveness, which it were well for them to follow. It was not that he loved the South less, but his duty to God more.

He was a devoted member of the Episcopal Church, but most liberal in his sentiments to other sects. An anecdote is told of a Jewish soldier who, during the last day of the army near Petersburg, asked a furlough that he might go to Richmond to attend the feast of the Passover. His captain endorsed on the paper, "If all these applications are granted, we shall have the whole army turning shaking Quakers."

General Lee sent back the petition with a kind note to the soldier, regretting that the exigencies of the times prevented his acceding to a request so natural and proper. Below the endorsement he wrote: "We should always have charity for those who differ from us in religion, and give every man all the aid in our power to keep the requirements of his faith."

We find several instances related of his delicacy in giving reproof, which also exhibits his quiet humor. "Late one night, he had occasion to go into a tent where several officers were sitting around a table, on which was a stone jug and two tin cups, busily engaged in the discussion of a mathematical problem. The General obtained the information he desired, gave a solution of the problem, and retired, the officers hoping that he had not noticed the jug. The next day, one of the officers, in presence of the others, related to General Lee a very strange dream he had had the night before. "That is not at all surprising," replied General Lee; 'when young gentlemen discuss at midnight mathematical problems, the unknown quantities of which are a stone jug and two tin cups, they may expect to have strange dreams'."*

Upon one occasion, while inspecting the lines near Petersburg, with several general officers, he asked General —— if a certain work, which he had directed him to complete as soon as possible, had been finished. General —— looked rather confused, but said that it was. General Lee at once proposed to ride in that direction. On getting to the place, he found that no progress had been made on the work since he was last there. General —— apologized, and said that he had not been on that part of the line for some time, but that Captain —— had told him that the work was completed, General Lee made no reply, but not long after began to compliment General —— on the horse he rode.

"Yes, sir," replied General ——, "he is a very fine animal. He belongs to my wife."

"A remarkably fine horse," replied General Lee, "but not a safe one for Mrs. ——. He is too mettlesome by far, and you ought to take the mettle out of him before you permit her to ride him. And let me suggest, General, that an admirable way to do that is to rule him a good deal along these trenches." The face of the gallant General —— turned crimson, and General Lee's eyes twinkled with mischief. No further allusion was made to the matter; but General —— adopted the suggestion.

The admirable control which he exercised over the army, was probably, in a great measure, owing to his self-control. The habits of self-restraint and self-denial, which he formed so early in life, were most important attributes of his great character. It is said that he never yielded to passion or impulse in dealing with his officers or men. Courtesy and urbanity ever marked his intercourse with them, and though firm, he was always tender-hearted and sympathetic, merciful and just.

Notes

* Miss Mason's Popular Life of General Lee.

* Miss Mason.

CHAPTER XX. LEE IS INVITED TO THE PRESIDENCY OF WASHINGTON COLLEGE, AND ACCEPTS THE POSITION.

DURING the spring and summer of 1865, General Lee had kindness extended to him with unparalleled generosity. It is said that estates were offered to him in England and Ireland, which he most courteously declined. He also declined the place of commercial agent of the South in New York, which would have proved lucrative in the extreme, preferring to share the broken fortunes of his native State. In the summer of that year he accepted the invitation of a lady to take his family to her house in Powhatan County for the summer. While there, an invitation was extended to him by the Trustees of Washington College, Lexington, Virginia, to become the President of that institution. To this invitation General Lee made the following characteristic reply:

POWHATAN COUNTY, August 24th, 1865.

GENTLEMEN:— I have delayed for some days replying to your letter of the 5th instant informing me of my election, by the Board of Trustees, to the Presidency of Washington College, from a desire to give the subject due consideration. Fully impressed with the responsibilities of the office, I have feared that I should be unable to discharge its duties to the satisfaction of the Trustees, or to the benefit of the country. The proper education of youth requires not only great ability, but, I fear, more strength than I now posses; for I do not fuel able to undergo the labor of conducting classes in regular courses of instruction. I could not, therefore, undertake more than the general administration and supervision of the institution.

There is another subject which I think worthy of the consideration of the Board. Being excluded from the terms of amnesty in the proclamation of the United States of the 29th of May last, and an object of censure to a portion of the country, I have thought it probable that my occupation of the position of president might draw upon the college a feeling of hostility, and I should therefore cause injury to an institution which it would be my highest object to advance.

I think it the duty of every citizen, in the present condition of the country, to do all in his power to aid in the restoration of peace and harmony, and in no way to oppose the police of the State or general Government directed to that object. It is particularly incumbent on those charged with the instruction of the young to set them an example of submission to authority, and I could not consent to be the cause of animadversion upon the college. Should you, however, take a different view, and think that my services, in the position tendered by the Board, will be advantageous to the college and the country, I will yield to your judgment and accept it; otherwise I must respectfully decline the offer.

Begging you to express to the Trustees of the college my heartfelt gratitude for the honor conferred upon me, and requesting you to accept my cordial thanks for the kind manner in which you have communicated its decision,

I am, gentlemen, your most obedient servant,

ROBERT E. LEE.
MESSRS. J. W. BROCKENBROUGH, Rector.
CH. McD. REID; ALFRED LEYBURN, HORATIO
THOMPSON, D.D, BOLIVAR CHRISTIAN, T. J. KIRKPATRICK, Committee.

The Trustees were but too much gratified to be able to overcome his scruples, so delicately expressed, and his installation into office took place on the 2d of October, 1865. The full account of the ceremonies has been thus described by a spectator:

General Robert E, Lee was to-day installed President of Washington College. There was no pomp or parade. The exercises of installation were the simplest possible; an exact compliance with the required formula of taking the oath by a new president, and nothing more. This was in accordance with the special request of General Lee. It was proposed to have the installation take place in the college chapel, to send invitations far and wide, to have a band of music to play enlivening airs, to have young girls robed in white and bearing chaplets of flowers, to sing songs of welcome, to have congratulatory speeches, to make it a holiday. That this programme was not carried out was a source of severe disappointment to many. But General Lee had expressed his wishes contrary to the choice and determination of the college Trustees and the multitude, and his wishes were complied with.

The installation took place at 9 A.M., in a recitation-room of the college. In this room were seated the Faculty and the students, the ministers of the town churches, a magistrate, and the county clerk; the last officials being necessary to the ceremonial. General Lee was ushered into the room by the Board of Trustees. Upon his entrance and introduction all in the room rose, bowed, and then resumed their seats. Prayer by the Rev. Dr. White, pastor of the Presbyterian Church, directly followed. To me it was a noticeable fact, and perhaps worthy of record, that he prayed for the President of the United States. Altogether, it was a most fitting and impressive prayer.

The prayer ended, Judge Brockenbrough, chairman of the Board of Trustees, stated the object of their coming together, to install General Lee as President of Washington College. He felt the serious dignity of the occasion, but it was a seriousness and dignity that should be mingled with heart-felt joy and gladness. Passing a brief eulogy upon General Lee, he congratulated the Board and College, and its present and future students, on having obtained one so loved, great, and worthy to preside over the college. General Lee remained standing, his arms quietly folded, calmly and steadfastly looking into the eyes of the speaker. Justice William White, at the instance of Judge Brockenbrough, now administered the oath of office to General Lee.

"For the benefit of those curious to know," adds the eye-witness," I will give the oath, to which General Lee subscribed, entire. It is as follows:

I do swear that I will, to the best of m y skill and judgment, faithfully and truly discharge the duties required of me by an Act entitled "An Act for incorporating the Rector and Trustees of Liberty Hall Academy," without favor, affection, or partiality: so help me God.

"To this oath General Lee at once affixed his signature, with the accompanying usual jurat of the swearing magistrate appended. The document was handed to the county clerk for safe and perpetual custodianship, and at the same time the keys of the college were given up by the Rector into the keeping of the new President.

"A congratulatory shaking of hands followed, which wound up the day's brief but pleasing, impressive, and memorable ceremonial. President Lee and those of the Trustees present, with the Faculty, now passed into the room set apart for the use of the President—a good-sized room, newly and very tastefully furnished.

"General Lee was dressed in a plain but elegant suit of gray. His appearance indicated the enjoyment of good health—better, I should say, than when he surrendered at Appomattox Court-House, the first and only occasion, before the present, of my having seen him."

The institution of which he had become President was a wreck, having been robbed of its library, torn and defaced during the war; but "Ambition had no charms for him, duty alone was his guide." It must have been a duty uncongenial to his tastes, and unsuited to the active habits of his life; but the army to him being a thing of the past, he determined that the remnant of his valuable life should not be wasted, but devoted to raising his stricken country, by training its youth in the paths of religion, literature, and honor.

When asked why he undertook this "brokendown institution," he calmly replied, "I have a mission to fulfil." And in fulfilling the mission he displayed the zest and ardor with which he had led his troops on the battle-field.

Though gentle and affectionate as a disciplinarian, he was very firm, being particularly careful that nothing like falsehood, dishonorable conduct, or disobedience to lawful authority should be overlooked. "The whole college," said one of the professors, "felt his influence," and his character was quietly yet irresistibly impressed upon it.

CHAPTER XXI. LEE'S MODE OF LIFE AT LEXINGTON, AND DEATH.

SOON after entering on the duties of the President of the college, he was offered, by the agent of an insurance company, its presidency, with a salary of ten thousand dollars. He told the agent that he could not give up his position in the college, and that he could not properly attend to both.

"But, General," said the agent, "we do not want you to discharge any duties. We simply wish the use of your name."

"Excuse me, sir," was his decided reply. "I cannot consent to receive pay for services I do not render."

But a short time before his death, a large manufacturing company in New York offered him a salary of fifty thousand dollars if he would become their president. He answered that his duty to the college fully occupied his time, and he could not receive pay where he did not render service. When the college wished to raise his salary, he would not allow it; and when the Trustees deeded to Mrs. Lee a house and an annuity of three thousand dollars, in Mrs. Lee's name, he respectfully declined it. "He declined all gratuities," says the Christian Observer; and though a loving people, for whom he had toiled so heroically, would most joyously have settled on him a handsome property, he preferred to earn his daily bread by his personal exertion, and to set to his people an example of honest industry."

As soon as Washington College was blessed by such a head, it became (except the University of Virginia) the most popular place in the South for the education of young men, who were attracted thither by his great name. Many of them doubtless had been led by him on the field of battle, and were proud to be led by him in the paths of literature. He entered upon his duties most heartily, and became deeply interested in each and every one of the students. To an old comrade in arms he wrote: "I am charmed with the duties of civil life."

"He found the college," wrote one of the professors, after his death, "practically bankrupt, disorganized, deserted; he left it rich, strong, and crowded with students." "Had this been the profession of his life," says the same professor, "General Lee would have been as famous among college presidents as he is now among soldiers."

He was personally very popular among the students. He labored for their advancement in all that was good and great in mind and character, day after day and year after year, and it is scarcely necessary to add how much they loved him. His "General Orders," as the boys called them, were always respected and obeyed. They were couched in the most courteous and gentle terms, which came to the hearts of the students with a persuasiveness that they could not resist. The one quoted below is a specimen.

WASHINGTON COLLEGE, Nov. 26, 1866.

The Faculty desire to call the attention of the students to the disturbances which occurred in the streets of Lexington on the nights of Friday and Saturday last. They believe that none can contemplate them with pleasure, or can find any reasonable grounds for their justification. These acts are said to have been committed by students of the College, with the apparent object of disturbing the peace and quiet of a town whose inhabitants have opened their doors for their reception and accommodation, and who are always ready to administer to their comfort and pleasure.

It requires but little consideration to see the error of such conduct, which could only have proceeded from thoughtlessness and a want of reflection. The Faculty therefore appeal to the honor and self-respect of the students to prevent any similar occurrence, trusting that their sense of what is due to themselves, their parents, and the institution to which they belong, will be move effectual in teaching them what is right and manly, than anything they can say.

There is one consideration connected with these disorderly proceedings, which the Faculty wish to bring to your particular notice; the example of your conduct, and the advantage taken of it by others, to commit outrages for which you have to bear the blame. They therefore exhort you to adopt the only course capable of shielding you from such charges—the effectual prevention of all such occurrences in future.

R. E. LEE,

President of Washington College.

Nothing could have been more kind and parental than such communications to students who felt that they deserved severe censure; and is it wonderful that they should have looked on him with a veneration little short of idolatry? With what satisfaction must the students who had the privilege of being under his Christian influence during those five years, look back to the time of their sojourn at Washington College. How blessed may have been his teaching and example to those who were willing to profit by them; their children may rise up to call him blessed, and the effect of his pure and undefiled religion be handed down from generation to generation.

The Rev. J. Wm. Jones, though not of the same denomination of Christians, had many opportunities, while a chaplain in the army, to observe and admire General Lee's deep and unaffected piety. After the war he resided in Lexington, and being frequently thrown with him, he seemed still more deeply impressed with his simple earnestness and devotion to the cause of religion.

After the death of General Lee, he published in the newspapers an interesting sketch of his religious life, in which he says, "With the close of the war, and the afflictions which came upon the country, the piety of this great man seems to have mellowed and deepened. The wiser could fill pages about his life at Lexington, and the bright evidence he gave of vital, active godliness. His place in the chapel and in his own church was never vacant, unless he was kept away by sickness. He was a constant reader and diligent student of the Bible. He was a most liberal contributor to his church and to other objects of benevolence. And then his manner of giving was so modest and unostentatious. In handing the writer a very handsome contribution to the 'Lexington Baptist Church Building Fund,' he quietly said, 'Will you do me the kindness to hand this to your treasurer, and save me the trouble of hunting him up? I am getting old now, and you young men must help me.' And his whole manner was that of one receiving, not bestowing a favor.

"General Lee was not accustomed to talk of his religious feelings; yet he would, when occasion offered, speak most decidedly of his reliance for salvation upon the merits of his Redeemer, and none who heard him could doubt for a moment that his faith was built on the 'Rock of Ages.' He manifested the deepest concern for the spiritual welfare of the young men under his care. Soon after becoming President of the College, he said, with deep feeling, to the Rev. Dr. White, the venerable pastor of the Presbyterian Church, 'I shall be disappointed, sir, and I shall fail in the leading object that brought me here, unless these young men become real Christians; and I wish you, and others of your sacred profession, to do all that you can to accomplish it.'

"At the beginning of each session he was accustomed to address a letter to the pastors of the town, inviting them to conduct the chapel service, and urging them to do all in their power for the spiritual good of the students. At the 'Concert of Prayer for Colleges,' in Lexington, last year, the writer made an address, in which he urged that the great need of our colleges was a genuine revival—that this could only come from God; and that inasmuch as He had promised His Holy Spirit to those who ask it, we should mike special prayer for a revival in the colleges of the country, and particularly in Washington College and the Virginia Military Institute. At the close of the meeting, General Lee came to me and said, with more than his usual warmth, 'I wish, sir, to thank you for that address. It was just what we needed. Our great want is a revival which shall bring these young men to Christ.'

"During the great revival in the Military Institute two years ago, he said to his pastor, 'This is the best news I have heard since I have been in Lexington. Would that we could have such a revival in all of our colleges.'

"Rev. Dr. Kirkpatrick, Professor of Moral Philosophy in Washington College, relates the following conversation that he had with Gen. Lee a short time previous to his death. We had been conversing for some time respecting the religious welfare of the students. Gen. Lee's feelings soon became so intense that for a time his utterance was choked; but recovering himself, with his eyes overflowing with tears, his lips quivering with emotion, and both hands raised, he exclaimed, 'Oh, Doctor! if I could only know that all these young men in the college were good Christians, I should have nothing more to desire.'

"Although General Lee was sincerely attached to the church of his choice, yet his large heart took in Christians of every name. He treated the ministers of all denominations with the most marked courtesy and respect, and not a few will cordially echo the remark of the venerable Dr. White, who said with deep feeling, during the memorial, 'He belonged to one branch of the church and I to another; yet in my intercourse with him,—an intercourse rendered far more frequent and intimate by the tender sympathy he felt in my ill health, the thought never occurred to me that we belonged to different churches. His love for the truth, and for all that is good and useful, was such as to render his brotherly kindness and charity as boundless as were the wants and sorrows of the race.' We could," continues Mr. Jones, "easily multiply incidents, and write more on the religious character of our beloved and honored chieftain, but the above must suffice."

Thus he seems to have impressed all good men, of every denomination, with feelings of admiration and love for his deep piety and genuine love for all Christians of every name. He was a devoted Episcopalian, but, with the truly catholic spirit of the large-hearted follower of Christ, he did not love other churches less for loving his own more.

The Rev. J. W. Jones tells another characteristic anecdote of his venerated friend:

Not long before the evacuation of Petersburg, Mr. J. was distributing tracts along the trenches, when General Lee, accompanied by General J. B. Gordon, General A. P. Hill, and other general officers, with their staffs, approached. They were inspecting our lines and reconnoitring those of the enemy. The keen eye of General Gordon recognized, and his cordial grasp detained, the humble tract distributor, as he warmly inquired about his work. General Lee at once reined in his horse and joined in the conversation; the rest of them gathered around, and the colporteur thus became the centre of a group of whose notice the highest princes of the earth might be proud. General Lee asked if we ever had calls for prayer-books, and said that if we would come to his headquarters, he would give us some for distribution. That a friend in Richmond had given him a new prayer-book, and upon his saying that he would give his old one, that he had used ever since the Mexican War, to some soldier, the friend had offered him a dozen new books for his old one; and he had, of course, accepted so good an offer, and now had twelve instead of one to give away, We called at the appointed hour. The General had gone out oil some important business, but (even amid his pressing duties) he had left the prayer-books with a member of his staff, with instructions concerning them. He had written on the fly-leaf, 'Presented by R. E. Lee;' and we are sure that the gallant men who received them, and who have survived the war, will cherish them as precious legacies, and hand them down as heirlooms in their families.

The Rev, T. U. Dudley, in his "Memorial Address" in Baltimore, speaks of an incident which occurred during a general review, which, like everything which is told of him, shows his veneration for sacred things, and his tender consideration for the feelings of others. It was near Winchester, in the bleak winter of 1862. The review had been ordered by General Lee. "One of those sad reviews," says Mr. Dudley, "which we all so well remember—so sad, and yet so necessary to the discipline of the army. There were no bright trappings, nor glitter of gold; the only glitter was the fire of determination in brave men's eyes. But all would appear in their best. There was a chaplain who, in obedience, as he believed, to this order, put on the pure white robe of his office and went to the review. Doubtless he heard the derisive laugh, the sneering remarks of those about him; but when the command he marched with passed the great chief, lifting his hat, he sad, 'I salute the Church of God.' The eye that was busy inspecting the accoutrements, the arms, the troops in which he trusted to do the work he had to do, could see the chaplain's robe. The commander, who sat in the immovable majesty we can remember so well, bent his uncovered head to salute the Church of the God he served."

A late writer in Blackwood's Magazine pronounces General Lee the "greatest soldier, with two exceptions, that any English-speaking nation ever produced." Were Marlborough and Wellington regarded as his superiors, or was our own Washington one of the exceptions? We know not; we are not portraying General Lee as a military man, but as a soldier of Christ. In that character he has passed through a long, active life; surrounded by the snares and temptations of the camp; exposed to the most harrowing trials and disappointments, and finally he became the victim to the most cruel overthrow of his dearest hopes. And yet his conduct seemed almost blameless. With clean hands and a pure heart he trod his thorny path, giving evidence, by his daily walk and conversation, that he was led by the Spirit of God; for, in the language of President Davis, "this good citizen, this gallant soldier, this great general, this true patriot, had yet a higher praise,—he was a true Christian."

However it may be regretted by his biographer that he was undemonstrative, and has left few incidents to record of his religious experience; yet we cannot closely contemplate his Christian character without feeling how beautiful and consistent it was in all its parts; how closely he walked with God; how in joy he found "delight in praise, and in sorrow sought relief in prayer." His bright example remains the praise of the whole earth, and to bless his countrymen to the remotest generation. But he is not—for God took him.

On the evening of the 28th of September, 1870, after a morning of great fatigue, he presided at a vestry meeting of Grace Church, Lexington, of which he was a member. After taking part in the meeting, he returned home in his usual health. On being summoned to tea, he walked to the table, and the family waited for him to ask a blessing on the meal—which had always been his habit in his family and in the camp; but his parted lips uttered no sound. He sank back into his chair, from which he was carried to his bed. The physicians at once pronounced the disease congestion of the brain.

For many days his family and friends surrounded his bed, praying and hoping for one trace of improvement, for one ray of returning reason. The intelligence quickly spread through the whole country, filling every heart with anxiety. The alternations between hope and fear continued but a few days. There was no decided return of reason. He muttered of the battle-field. Among his last words were: "Strike my tent! Send for Hill!"*

On the 12th of October, at nine o'clock in the morning, the ransomed spirit of General Lee entered into its eternal rest. Of the grief which pervaded the South, when the sad intelligence was transmitted to every part of the country by telegraph, it is needless to speak. The tolling of bells, flags at half-mast, public meetings, mourning badges, marked in every portion of the South that a dread calamity bad come over its people. Tears flowed abundantly in thousands of Southern homes; everywhere houses were draped with mourning; and, indeed, sorrow spread her pall over the land!

The Virginia Legislature immediately passed resolutions expressive of the general distress, and requesting that the remains of General Lee might be brought to Hollywood Cemetery, near Richmond, for interment. His family, however, preferred that his remains should rest at the scene of his last labors, and beneath the chapel of Washington College they were accordingly interred.

On the 13th, his body was borne to the college chapel, escorted by a guard composed of Confederate soldiers. Next to the hearse, "Traveller,"* the faithful gray that had borne him to so many battle-fields, was led. The Trustees and Faculty of the college, the students, and cadets of the Military Institute, and the citizens, followed in procession. Above the chapel floated the flag of Virginia draped in mourning. Through this and the succeeding day, the body, covered with flowers, lay in state, visited by thousands who came to look for the last time upon his noble features.

On Friday, the 15th, the last rites were performed, amid the tolling of bells, the thundering of cannon, and the sound of martial music.

The students of the college, officers and soldiers of the Confederate army, and about a thousand persons, assembled at the chapel. A military escort, with the officers of General Lee's staff, were in the front. The hearse followed, with "Traveller" close behind it. Next came a committee of the Virginia Legislature, with citizens from all parts of the State. Passing the Military Institute, the cadets made the military salute as the body appeared, then joined the procession, and escorted it back to the chapel. The procession was more than a mile long. After the first salute, a gun was fired every three minutes. Moving still to the sound of martial music, the procession re-entered the grounds of Washington College and was halted in front of the chapel. The coffin was removed to the rostrum. Emblems of mourning met the eye in every direction. Feminine affection had hung garlands of flowers on the pillars and walls. Thousands were present, many surrounding the chapel.

General Lee had requested that no funeral sermon should be preached over his body. The funeral service of the Episcopal Church was impressively read by his pastor, the Rev. William N. Pendleton, D.D. The coffin was then carried by the pall-bearers to the library room in the basement of the chapel, where it was lowered into the vault prepared for its reception. The funeral services were concluded in the open air by prayer, and singing General Lee's favorite hymn:

How firm a foundation, ye saints of the Lord,
Is laid for your faith in His excellent word.

The sorrowful multitude then separated, and slowly returned to their own homes.

Blessed are the dead who die in the Lord: even so saith the Spirit; for they rest from their labors.

Notes

* Remarkably coincident with the dying words of his "great Lieutenant," Jackson, whose last word, were: "Let A. P. Hill prepare for action! March the infantry rapidly to the front! Let us cross the river and rest under he shade of the trees."

* "Traveller" survived his master but a few months.